Cambridge Elements ≡

Elements in Defence Economics
edited by
Keith Hartley
University of York

THE POLITICAL ECONOMY OF GULF DEFENSE ESTABLISHMENTS

Zoltan Barany
University of Texas

T0329143

CAMBRIDGE
UNIVERSITY PRESS

CAMBRIDGE
UNIVERSITY PRESS

University Printing House, Cambridge CB2 8BS, United Kingdom

One Liberty Plaza, 20th Floor, New York, NY 10006, USA

477 Williamstown Road, Port Melbourne, VIC 3207, Australia

314–321, 3rd Floor, Plot 3, Splendor Forum, Jasola District Centre,
New Delhi – 110025, India

79 Anson Road, #06–04/06, Singapore 079906

Cambridge University Press is part of the University of Cambridge.

It furthers the University's mission by disseminating knowledge in the pursuit of
education, learning, and research at the highest international levels of excellence.

www.cambridge.org
Information on this title: www.cambridge.org/9781108959759
DOI: 10.1017/9781108961820

© Zoltan Barany 2021

First published 2021

A catalogue record for this publication is available from the British Library.

ISBN 978-1-108-95975-9 Paperback
ISSN 2632-332X (online)
ISSN 2632-3311 (print)

The Political Economy of Gulf Defense Establishments

Elements in Defence Economics

DOI: 10.1017/9781108961820
First published online: January 2021

Zoltan Barany
University of Texas

Author for correspondence: Zoltan Barany, barany@austin.utexas.edu

Abstract: The six monarchies on the Arabian Peninsula have devoted enormous sums to defense in past decades. Nevertheless, the gap between their expensive armaments and their capacity to deter aggression and/or project military strength has narrowed very little in that time. This Element takes a political economy approach and argues that structural factors inherent in the Gulf states' political systems prohibit civilian oversight of the defense sector and are responsible for this outcome. Lax restraints on military outlays, in turn, enable widespread corruption, lead to large-scale waste, and account for the purchasing of unneeded, unsuitable, and incompatible weapons systems. The Element explores the challenges caused by plummeting oil prices and the resulting budget cuts and considers the development of domestic defense industries in Saudi Arabia and the UAE, intended as a part of their economic diversification program. The setbacks of the Saudi-led coalition's ongoing war in Yemen starkly illustrate the narrative.

Keywords: Arabian Gulf, Gulf Cooperation Council, defense sector, political economy, corruption

ISBNs: 9781108959759 (PB), 9781108961820 (OC)
ISSNs: 2632-332X (online), 2632–3311 (print)

Contents

1 Introduction

The economics of the military establishments of the Gulf Cooperation Council (GCC) states (Bahrain, Kuwait, Oman, Qatar, Saudi Arabia, and the United Arab Emirates [UAE]) are chronically understudied. This work aims to begin filling this lacuna in the scholarly literature. Given the socio-political and socio-cultural complexities and attributes of civil-military relations and defense economics in the region, an analysis of "simple demand-and-supply market activity" could not do justice to this subject; therefore, I adopt a political economy approach instead (Wahid 2009: 14).

1.1 Research Questions and Arguments

The extant literature on the defense and security affairs of the GCC is still sparse, even though the political and economic clout and strategic weight of the six Gulf monarchies have steadily increased in recent decades. All too often, general studies on the Middle East and North Africa (MENA) still ignore the states on the Arabian Peninsula or fail to recognize the significant differences between Arab monarchies and republics. From the perspective of military-security issues, the most important disparity between them is that, in contrast to republics, in monarchies the military as an institution has not played a political let alone state-building role, the generals' political influence has been negligible, and the GCC armies' officers have not been involved in their national economies.

This Element seeks to answer several fundamental questions. What political imperatives have guided the development of Gulf armed forces? Insofar as the public's ability to influence military expenditure is highly limited, what are the primary factors that explain the patterns of military expenditure in the Gulf states? What have been the macroscopic trends in Gulf defense budgets since 2011? What is the nature of the Gulf states' domestic defense industries, and what factors account for the intra-Gulf variation in these industries?

In recent decades, the GCC states' weapons acquisition programs have represented a massively disproportionate share of global arms purchases, and in per capita terms, the Gulf region has the highest military spending in the world. Paradoxically, their military performance has been weak, most recently demonstrated by Saudi Arabia's inept performance in the Yemen Civil War (2015–). Some reasons for the Gulf armies' ineffectiveness are found in socio-cultural causes, but several stem from political-structural and economic sources. This Element will seek to understand what aspects of defense economics can be said to be responsible for this great disparity between defense spending and military performance.

1.1.1 Key Points and Arguments

The unique configuration of geopolitical, social, and economic circumstances faced by the Gulf countries have spawned an unusual set of military institutions and practices that merit exposition. In particular, they have extremely high levels of military spending and there is very little oversight that regulates the states' defense outlays, which together yield an inefficient and underperforming military.

This Element advances four broad arguments. First, the Gulf countries' geographical and natural endowments act as a double-edged sword: on the one hand, their strategic position and abundant fossil-fuel resources allow them to realize high living standards; on the other hand, these attributes also make them vulnerable to security threats from inside and outside the region. Therefore, they are characterized by a large latent demand for military spending, combined with a high capacity to spend militarily, especially on a per-capita basis. The Gulf states' defense budgets, already enormous for the size of their territory and population, have increased faster in the 2010s than in any other region of the world – despite the challenges of declining oil prices, growing populations, and a host of additional troubling economic problems – responding to the security challenges signified by the Arab Spring and the (perceived) growing threat from Iran.

Second, owing to their socio-political structures, the ability of the public in Arabia to exercise control over the size and nature of military spending is essentially nonexistent. In these absolute monarchies, there is little popular representation and the only limitation on the rulers' policies comes, if at all, from within the royal family itself. In other words, only the ruling family enjoys control over the amount of resources and the manner in which they are expended on defense and security. The consequence of this lack of civilian oversight tends to be high levels of corruption, which reinforces the latent demand for military spending. In many political systems, weapons acquisition creates broad opportunities for large-scale embezzlement. Some of the Gulf's ruling families have amply utilized these occasions for fraudulent transactions. At the same time, it must be noted, Arabia is by no means one of the world's most corrupt regions.

Third, the lack of oversight also distorts incentives in military procurement. Rather than a pragmatic response to actual needs relating to national defense, political calculation and institutional and/or individual vanity have often motivated or even determined defense spending patterns in general and armaments acquisitions in particular. The second and third arguments point at political-structural factors that contribute to and help explain the ineffectiveness and general underperformance of Arabia's armies.

Fourth and finally, the desert climates and political development paths of the Gulf countries have combined to leave their domestic industrial capacity weakened in all domains. Consequently, their military spending is dominated by foreign purchases, with extremely limited domestic defense industries. To offset this long-term reliance on the world armament market, in recent years Saudi Arabia and the UAE have pursued a program of indigenous military manufacturing. The different approaches of the two governments to developing their domestic defense industry reflect the disparities in their overall strategies toward economic and military-security development.

1.1.2 Road Map to This Element

This Element proceeds in six parts. In the next section, I will consider the political system of Gulf monarchies as it is indispensable to understanding the ways in which their defense establishments are developed and managed. The third segment focuses on the Gulf Cooperation Council and explores why it has not succeeded in realizing meaningful collaboration between its six members in economic, political, and military realms. The following part begins with a brief look at the Gulf states' overall economic health, relays the challenges they have faced in recent years, analyzes the burden of defense spending, and then traces the huge increases in their military outlays, particularly since 2011. Next, I focus on what type of armaments Gulf states purchase, from whom, and why, and explore the issue of corruption that all too often accompanies defense procurement. The penultimate part is devoted to a brief look at the issues of weapons and facilities maintenance and expansion, and explore the development of domestic defense industries. In the concluding section, I explore the negative effects of the Gulf states' defense economic attributes on their armies' performances in Yemen and reassess the arguments.

2 The Domestic Political Environment

The Gulf monarchies are authoritarian systems that fit comfortably into H. E. Chehabi and Juan Linz's conceptualization of the "sultanistic" regime subtype (Chehabi and Linz 1998). Gulf rulers allow virtually no political debate, embrace what may well be described as "cult of personality," and their power is anything but well-defined; "in all the world perhaps only the monarchs of Swaziland and Bhutan hold" as much power as the Gulf royals (Lucas 2004:104). The political systems of the Gulf are quite simple, dependent as they are on individuals rather than institutions.

2.1 Family States

When contemplating the Gulf ruling families' hold over the state, it is hard not to invoke Louis XIV's immortal declaration (*"L'État c'est moi!"*) that has depicted absolute monarchies ever since. To be sure, the royal families of the Gulf are constrained by some "soft factors" such as Islamic norms (i.e., ruling as Islam requires), attention to consensus building, and including family members and other elites in the formulation of decision-making. Still, they view themselves as the owners rather than the rulers of their countries. This attitude may be unseemly, but it is hardly unwarranted. In many respects, they are, even now, like the medieval king, who, as Reinhard Bendix explains, "governed his country like a giant household. There [is] little distinction between public revenue and income derived from the royal domains . . . . Members of the royal family participated in affairs of state as a matter of hereditary right" (Bendix 1980: 248). The Gulf kings' purported proprietorship of their realm helps distinguish their reign from those of the Arab republics' strongmen.

In the Gulf monarchies, no decision of consequence is made and no policy is devised, let alone implemented, without the rulers' agreement. They make laws that need not be justified, for the rulers are not accountable to anyone, even if they consult family members and advisers. If there is some sort of pseudo-parliament in the country, it may "enact" these laws, but that endeavor is really just a nicety, a charade, because the very existence of a legislative organ is at the mercy of the ruler – even Kuwait's National Assembly, a partial exception in Arabia's mostly toothless representative bodies. The laws are put into effect and enforced by institutions whose staff collectively and individually serve at the pleasure of the monarch. All power in the land flows from the ruler: first to members of the royal family, then to preferred clans, tribes, approved religious authorities, important business families, and a wide range of individuals. The state can and does punish citizens with impunity, whether innocent or guilty, with any penalty or retribution it sees fit.

The royal families are the essential core of the absolute state. They tend to be unusually large by the standards of non-Arab monarchies; just how large varies according to how the family is defined. The most expansive is Saudi Arabia's Al Saud family; the kingdom's founder, Ibn Saud, had more than 40 sons and even more daughters. Depending on who is doing the counting, the royal family includes between 15,000 and 30,000 princes and princesses (Kulish and Mazzetti, 2016; Kéchichian, 2001). Even the Al Khalifa, tiny Bahrain's ruling family, has approximately 3,000 to 5,000 members of different status and in various branches, making up 0.43 to 0.72 percent of the country's 689,000 citizens.[1] The smallest is Oman's Al Said clan; its royal family has only 85 male descendants with both Omani parents who could be considered the legitimate heirs of the late Sultan Qaboos. Marriages between the royal families of the Gulf are common; these unions strengthen relationships and alliances across Arabia. It is important to understand that in a royal family of thousands, only a small proportion of princes are truly influential. In a small country like Kuwait, with a citizenry of 1.2 million, at most a few dozen princes are prominent; in the much larger Saudi context, there are probably several hundred. Of course, being an Al Sabah in Kuwait, an Al Thani in Qatar, or an Al Maktoum in Dubai confers privileges, prestige, and *wasta* (pull, clout, connections), but this does not necessarily mean that a person is excessively wealthy or enjoys great influence.

One crucial area where royal blood consistently pays dividends is the labor market, especially for public sector positions. Gulf rulers exercise their power through their entire extended families. These family members are the top clients of their royal patron, whose loyalty needs to be reinforced and guaranteed by perquisites and benefits, such as well-remunerated employment that often requires modest exertion. The vast majority of key jobs in government and the judiciary, as well as broad swathes of the economy, are held by members of the royal family or, to a lesser extent, influential tribal leaders who have long been associated with them. This is even more true for positions of strategic significance or sensitivity.

The most consequential of these are in the monarchies' defense sector. The ministries of defense, interior, and foreign affairs are almost always headed by royal family members; these men – and occasionally, though still very rarely, women – also have first dibs on top jobs in these ministries. Such appointments include deputy and assistant ministerships, department headships, and in the foreign ministry, ambassadorships to important allies, powerful countries, and trading partners. The most sensitive command positions or those in high-profile combat units in the state's coercive apparatus are usually held by royal family members.

The ruler typically has a number of sons and nephews, and royal families tend to have several branches. The ambitions of the sons and the goodwill, allegiance, and aspirations of the leaders of other branches to the ruler and his family need to be buttressed and satisfied with prominent and lucrative public sector positions. This is one of the main reasons for the proliferation of government offices and departments and, in the defense-security sector, of

---

[1] Interview with a Bahraini demographer (Manama, December 3, 2015). The population number is from 2019.

new agencies and organizations. The primary and most binding allegiance of the people in these jobs is to the ruler from whom, directly or indirectly, they have received them. Since they operate in a system that is akin to a large family enterprise, their loyalty is not to an institution – say, the constitution or parliament or even a ministry – but to the head of the royal family. In a system like this, loyalty to the ruling family and personal connections are more imperative than aptitude or suitability. This absence of meritocracy is one of the fundamental reasons for the ineffectiveness of the Gulf states' institutions, including their armed forces.

2.2 Centralization and Absolutism

A key attribute of autocracies is the centralization or even "hyper-centralization" of authority in the hands of the king and his closest family members. In the absolute monarchies of the Gulf, this trait is reinforced by inflated deference to authority, passivity, and conformity. This deference to authority is, indeed, the flipside of the centralization of authority and the reluctance to devolve power and delegate responsibility (Pollack 2019: 378). Decisions are made by an extremely small circle of people. For instance, in the UAE, the Crown Prince, Mohammed bin Zayed (a.k.a. MbZ), and his closest advisers make most decisions, even on issues that a colonel or brigadier would resolve in the US, the UK, or Israel. More generally, hyper-centralized decision-making, overlapping jurisdictions of central and local governments, and other bureaucratic challenges often cause the failure to put ambitious public policies, such as Saudi Crown Prince Mohammed bin Salman's (a.k.a. MbS) Vision 2030, into action.

Furthermore, even at the top of institutional hierarchies, information tends to be compartmentalized and areas of competence and responsibility are carefully guarded because they are a source of power, guaranteeing one's continued relevance. "A veteran of Pentagon turf wars," an American observer wrote, "will feel like a kindergartner when he encounters the rivalries that exist in the Arab military headquarters" (De Atkine 2000: 21). Even senior bureaucrats and military officers often know little outside of their narrow specialization and tend not to take advantage of opportunities that present themselves and not demonstrate personal initiative for fear of making a mistake or possibly stepping on the toes of a superior. Moreover, if possible, even relatively high-ranking defense officials tend to avoid or put off making decisions because of qualms about potentially overstepping boundaries.

And yet this setup of an absolute monarchy – resting on the pillars of oil revenue, tribalism, religious and business establishments, and a coercive apparatus – has served the Gulf kingdoms well. While the constitutional monarchies the British bequeathed to Egypt and Iraq lasted only a few decades, the absolute monarchies of Arabia have had no major challenges to their survival. It is no wonder why Gulf rulers reject calls from their feeble opposition to embark on reforms – such as a popularly elected legislature that would bring the public into the decision-making process – that could lead to enhanced political participation and, in time, to constitutional monarchies. For, from the rulers' perspective, the arrangements required by a genuine constitutional monarchy would introduce a large number of variables into the equation that would only weaken their hold on power.

To be sure, there are some differences in just how absolute the rule of Gulf monarchs is. At one end of the spectrum is Kuwait, where the royal family tends to devolve a measure of decision-making authority to the National Assembly. Bahrain did have genuine elections in the past (1973, 2002, 2010), but the opposition boycotted the 2014 contest and the last one, held in 2018, was little more than a farce (Al Ghanim 2010). Placed toward the other end of the scale are Qatar, the UAE, and Saudi Arabia, where citizens enjoy virtually no genuine political representation, although each of these states maintains a Consultative Assembly or some kind of ostensibly representative body. Oman's long-reigning late Sultan Qaboos probably concentrated more power in his hand than any of his peers in Arabia, though he, too, granted some choice to citizens to choose from candidates, preselected by the state, for the Consultative Assembly, the lower house of the Council of Oman.

The bottom line is that in Arabia, all reforms targeting liberalization or changes permitting a modicum of popular participation are easily reversible and are entirely at the pleasure of the rulers. A salient example is the 2018 "reform" in Saudi Arabia that lifted the ban on female drivers – the only country in the world where people were prohibited from driving based on nothing but their gender. The point here is that Crown Prince Mohammed, as a representative of the Saudi state, granted this privilege to female citizens; in other words, it was a gift from the monarchy, not some long-denied right that women fought for and attained. From an outside perspective, it must have seemed bizarre that a number of women activists who campaigned for the right to drive were subsequently prosecuted, flogged, and jailed by the state. However, the ruler merely wanted to drive home the point that the reform was a result of his largesse, a demonstration of his munificence, rather than the outcome of the women's activism.

2.3 Threats to Stability

Historically, one of the major threats to the Gulf chieftains and monarchs has been assassination and coups within their own families. These dangers have been relatively rare in recent decades, though succession paths have not always been smooth. Currently five of the six GCC states' rulers are relatively young, and only Kuwait can expect a royal succession (its emir was born in 1929 and the crown prince is only eight years younger); the jockeying for power has already begun (Winder, 2020).

The Gulf countries are absolute monarchies, but their rulers, especially since the early 1990s, have intended to create a veneer of political participation and established various councils (municipal, regional, and national) and advisory bodies. Some of the members of these organizations are elected, though most are appointed. Three points are helpful to recognize. First, none of these bodies across Arabia have the authority to make and implement decisions against the wishes of the ruling family. Second, they are all expendable: when push comes to shove, they can be dissolved, abolished, or suspended at the ruler's whim. And third, they enjoy virtually no influence over defense-security matters. Political organizations that the government disapproves of are simply disbanded via court ruling, as was Bahrain's well-established Al-Wefaq National Islamic Society, a Shia Muslim party, in 2016.

Kuwait's National Assembly (NA) is the outlier in the Gulf states, as it possesses conventional legislative powers such as to debate and enact laws, oversee the budget process, and monitor government ministries and agencies (Herb 2004). Unlike elsewhere in the Gulf, where the defense budget is entirely in the hands of the ruling family and the executive branch, in Kuwait the NA must approve the budget, including its military outlays, once it is presented by the government. Even in Kuwait, though, the actual clout members of parliament enjoy over defense-related matters is extremely limited. The MPs understand that the government does not want to play politics with defense issues and are quite passive in this area.[2]

The Gulf monarchies have to contend with little domestic opposition that, at least to an outside observer, would represent a credible threat to their safety let alone survival. At the same time, the upheavals in 2011 frightened the ruling families into stepping up security measures against potential adversaries, no matter how improbable or weak the challenge they pose might be. As a result, we have witnessed a militarization of the Gulf in the last decade signaled by elevated defense budgets and armaments acquisition, stepped up joint exercise activity, and sharpening focus on counterterrorism. At the same time, some new policies have served the objective of deepening ideas of nationhood among Gulf citizens. For instance, mandatory military service was recently introduced in Qatar and the UAE and reintroduced in Kuwait, military parades have been

---

[2] Interview with a Kuwaiti political scientist (Kuwait City, December 13, 2016).

staged on national holidays, and military museums and memorials have been opened in several Gulf countries (Barany 2018).

The exception to the overall feebleness of Gulf opposition is Bahrain's majority Shia community that the state has systematically suppressed and marginalized for decades. The regime's heavy-handed sectarian crackdown had radicalized the opposition and pro-regime communities on both sides of the Shia-Sunni divide. At three to four million, Saudi Arabia's Shia population is far larger than Bahrain's, but it only makes up about 20 percent of the kingdom's citizenry. Therefore, it represents a more modest threat to stability, even though the Shia community predominantly dwells in the oil-rich Eastern Province.

Given their fixation with external threats, particularly the threat from Iran, Gulf states tend to conflate domestic and foreign security. Fear of terrorism (e.g., ISIS and Al-Qaeda affiliates) is of course one of the most important incentives for vigilance in the GCC (Haykel 2016; Fishman 2016). Terrorist threats are not merely academic: several Arabian states – Bahrain, Kuwait, Saudi Arabia – have been attacked in recent years. Saudi Arabia and Bahrain are also concerned about their territory turning into a scene of transnational Shia activism portending Iran's growing sway in the Gulf.

The UAE government's greatest fear has been Islamic radicalization and at the focus of its attention is the Islah movement, which has been traditionally influential in Ras al-Khaimah (RaK), Fujairah, and other northern emirates. In 2014, the UAE designated both the Muslim Brotherhood and Islah as terrorist organizations; the previous year, in tandem with Riyad, Abu Dhabi helped finance the toppling of Egypt's elected Muslim Brotherhood-dominated government. All GCC states view dissent unforgivingly, but the UAE, Saudi Arabia, and Bahrain quash it the most mercilessly. For instance, in 2018 Abu Dhabi convicted Matthew Hedges, a British scholar of espionage, and sentenced him to life in prison offering not a shred of evidence before freeing him owing to mounting international pressure (Hearst 2018). For decades, Saudi authorities have forcibly repatriated (i.e., abducted) their citizens, including disagreeable members of the royal family, from foreign countries if they misbehaved. One of the most effective ways the Gulf monarchies punish their undesirable nationals is by revoking their citizenship.

Most citizens of Arabia receive a strictly sanitized version of news about their countries' politics, economies, and social affairs. Press freedoms in the Gulf are heavily circumscribed. The "2019 World Press Freedom Index" of Reporters without Borders (RWB) makes the point that the media is anything but free in Arabia. RWB's ranking helpfully suggests the subtle differences between the six kingdoms. Out of 180 countries, Kuwait is ranked 108th in terms of press freedoms, Qatar is 128th, Oman is 132nd, the is UAE 133rd, Bahrain is 167th, and Saudi Arabia is 172nd (Reporters without Borders 2019).

2.4 The Monarchy and the Armed Forces

Institutional underdevelopment remains one of the most unmistakable characteristics of Arab monarchies. Although this trait may be somewhat less pronounced in the defense sector – owing to its regimented and hierarchical nature and British origins – than in other areas, the security apparatus of the Gulf states still displays a relatively low level of institutionalization and excessive reliance on and deference to personalities. As in most authoritarian states, the GCC armies' crucial mission is to be the regimes' last domestic line of defense versus its political foes. To be sure, the regular armed forces are seldom deployed against the people, and they do not ordinarily perform police functions. Nevertheless, if the various police and security organizations are unable to suppress a revolt, the military is called in to defend the regime with whatever means necessary.

Given the critical importance of the security sector to the survival of their regimes, the ruling families control the coercive apparatus even more closely than other segments of the state. Traditionally, in all of the oil monarchies, rulers have appointed sons, brothers, nephews, and uncles to military leadership positions. The vast majority of contemporary senior defense officials and commanders are members of the royal families or individuals closely connected to them by marriage, kinship, or tribal affiliation. One of the greatest weaknesses of Gulf armed forces is that they are not meritocracies. Therefore, it would be tempting to write off the many military commanders of royal blood as incompetent hacks. In fact, many – and probably an upward trending proportion – of the people who hold sensitive positions are capable. The royal families have an existential stake in the protection of their domain so, all things being equal, they want to choose the best available candidate.

"The most important factor that Middle Eastern monarchs must take into account in choosing their policies," Herb writes, "is the need to keep the army in the barracks" (Herb 1999: 231). The type of political-institutional relationship Gulf ruling families have adopted and advanced with their armed forces is one of the main reasons for the ineffectiveness of their armies. Perhaps the most typical attribute of the defense establishments of autocracies is that "the army" is actually several armed organizations. The fear of coups is manifested in the multiplication of parallel military forces. In fact, the rich Gulf countries have been able to develop multi-tiered defense establishments. The different military and paramilitary organizations are not only established to provide the ruling families (patrons) with a sense of security but also to furnish them with positions and perquisites that they can dole out to family members (clients). These jobs bestow on the princes a much-valued sense of status and purpose and binds them closer to the ruler. The regular armed forces are kept relatively small – with the one partial exception of Saudi Arabia's – and are counterbalanced by separate National Guards, special forces, security services, and other elements.

The Gulf armies are heavily politicized in the sense that their personnel must support the ruling families' policies and positions unquestioningly. In hierarchically structured organizations like the armed forces, politicization is a top-down issue and its greatest impact is felt on the highest levels of command. Politicization, the enforced political reliability of top commanders, is a major coup-proofing method in GCC armies. Coup-proofing may be thought of as "the set of actions a regime takes to prevent a military coup" (Quinlivan 1999: 133). Even top commanders are kept on a very short leash. The fact that Gulf armies play no independent political role is, in part, the success of politicization. In Saudi Arabia, Gaub argues, it is also the result of four intertwined dynamics: (1) distrustful attitude of the civic leadership leading to slow build-up of the armed forces; (2) creation of force from the ground meant that the officer corps was neither cohesive nor strong enough to oppose civilians; (3) the military's weaknesses prevented the rulers to deploy them fearing a fiasco; and (4) owing to its lacking combat history, the Saudi military evoked little sentiment and no political support for any potential political action (Gaub 2017: 155).

Gulf military establishments maintain regular armed forces – composed of the three conventional branches of the army, navy, and air force – that fulfill traditional roles. The key function of national guards, in the larger forces complemented by even more exclusive royal and/or presidential guards, is regime protection. The state closely controls and monitors these heavily compartmentalized armies. Any large-scale – which, in these armies means battalion-level or above – exercise of land forces is a potential threat to the government and, therefore, is carefully checked and observed, especially if live ammunition is being used (De Atkine 2000: 23). Often, one unit or branch of service will have a capability and another the counter-capability. Whether Gulf rulers face realistic coup threats is debatable, what matters is that they think they do. Therefore, they have adopted positions that limit the effectiveness of their forces. One obvious example is joint force operations – that is, campaigns in which different branches (army, navy, air force, etc.) of the armed forces must work together. This is a crucial element of modern warfare, but it is difficult to conduct in the atmosphere of institutional fragmentation, information compartmentalization, and personal and intra-organizational rivalry that exemplifies Gulf military affairs.

3 The GCC: The Unrealized Promise of Cooperation

Perhaps the most important point that jumps out at those studying the Gulf states' foreign affairs is their constant search for allies capable of protecting them. Although the six GCC member-states have raised 375,000 active-duty soldiers backed by some of the best equipment and facilities money can buy, they are poorly trained, divided, and unable to resist any possible regional aggressor for long. Rather than finding and building on common ground and emphasizing the many fundamental features that their polities, societies, and economies share, Gulf leaders have mired their regional organization in petty squabbles and have hung onto differences that deepened the rifts among them. It would be hard to find a six-country region anywhere in the world with more commonalities. And yet, aside from the fact that it was founded and has endured for four decades, in terms of substantive achievements, the GCC has been a lesson in failure.

3.1 Evolution and Devolution

The GCC was established in May 1981, and its survival for forty years *is* an achievement for an organization in such a difficult neighborhood and in such turbulent times. Although as a security organization the GCC has had few successes, in other respects it has chalked up some minor feats. Soon after its founding, the GCC reached a Unified Economic Agreement in 1981, a Custom Union in 2003, and the GCC Common Market in 2008. Like so many initiatives emanating from the GCC, on paper the Common Market and the Custom Union sound impressive, but they have not lived up to the generous appraisal of some analysts. In fact, without the necessary bureaucratic and standards alignments, much less the transportation infrastructure to support robust trade between the GCC countries, this customs and trade union, such as it is, is basically mean-ingless. The common currency and shared central banking apparatus that was proposed to be introduced by 2010 fell victim to political hurdles as well.

The GCC initiated a number of other projects that have yet to take shape, including power connectivity based on a common grid in certain areas. By exploiting extant tribal and clan networks throughout the Arabian Peninsula, the GCC has endowed its citizens with one important though less tangible or apparent benefit: a rhetorical and institutional alternative identity beyond that of the state, the *khaleeji* (i.e., Gulf Arab) identity (Bianco and Stansfield 2018: 624). The GCC has also encouraged economic and trade cooperation and standardization among its members and working together in these areas has spurred some partnerships and coordination in others as well. Still, the vast potential for economic cooperation has barely been touched mostly owing to bureaucratic infighting, turf wars, administrative inflexibility, and lacking commitment.

Since the Arab Spring, the GCC's weaknesses have become only more evident. Forty years after its founding, it is still unclear whether it is a collective security organization or a multilateral forum for greater economic, commercial, monetary, or diplomatic integration (Kamrava 2018: 80). To be sure, the member states are different in terms of the size of their populations, territories, economies, and their geostrategic positions but no more so than other regional alliances. What does set the GCC apart from other regional groupings is the reluctance on the part of its dominant power, Saudi Arabia, to comprom-ise, alleviate differences, use tact to resolve disputes, and occasionally sacrifice for the sake of the community. Even prior to the Arab Spring, however, GCC leaders – particularly from Oman, Qatar, and the UAE – repeatedly and openly disagreed with Saudi dictates. For instance, in 2009 when the GCC Monetary Council was established and a Saudi minister was selected for its director and Riyadh as the central bank's headquarters, the UAE quit the body rather than accept these conditions thereby reducing the chances of a common currency. Oman has been consistent in its disinclination to compromise its foreign policy independence.

Although the GCC's structure, small membership size, and institutional make-up allow for expedient mediation, disagreements had occasionally deteri-orated into hostile rhetoric and, at times, even into threats of military action. The organization's 1981 charter provides for a "Commission for the Settlement of Disputes" attached to the Supreme Council, but this body was never actually formed. When intra-GCC disputes have been resolved – such as boundary issues between Bahrain and Qatar (regarding the Hawar Islands) and the oil-rich neutral zone between Kuwait and Saudi Arabia – the outcome was reached either through mediation by other international organizations or bilateral nego-tiations (Wiegand 2012; Guzansky 2016).

In the absence of an effective internal dispute resolution mechanism, three of the six GCC members have often facilitated the settling of quarrels. Oman has been a widely recognized peacemaker and compromise facilitator in the region and farther afield. More recently, Qatar has also been instrumental in alleviating some conflicts in Chad, Iraq, Algeria, and elsewhere, though it received the most accolades from Washington for serving as an organizer of meetings that preceded the US-Taliban deal in 2020. Kuwait, too, has become a recognized mediator in Arabia. In late 2019, its emir called the persisting regional dispute between Saudi Arabia and its partners and Qatar "no longer acceptable or tolerable," but his admonitions fell on deaf ears (*Al Jazeera* 2019). This quarrel, in fact, may lead to the GCC's undoing.

3.2 The Conflict with Qatar

Qatar has never been happy about Riyadh's guidance of the GCC. Some Saudi leaders, among them the former Crown Prince, Mohammed bin Nayef, were able to accommodate Doha's ambitious foreign policy and mitigate the strains they caused. His replacement with the combustible MbS, however, virtually guaranteed surging tensions between Riyadh and Doha. Frictions between the GCC's hardliners (Saudi Arabia, the UAE, and Bahrain) and Qatar have intensified since the Arab Spring. Doha, notwithstanding its illiberal rule at home, embraced reform movements through sympathetic coverage in its Al Jazeera broadcasting network and substantial financial assistance. It has for long supported the Muslim Brotherhood and extended financial aid to Mohammed Morsi's government in Egypt, even in the face of strong Saudi and Emirati opposition to them.

Naturally, Qatar opposed Abdel Fattah al-Sisi's Saudi- and UAE-backed coup in 2013. The Gulf rivals also supported competing armed factions in Libya and Syria. Doha did not align its stance with the GCC hard-liners against what the latter labeled Islamist terrorist groups in the region. Joined by Egypt, they eventually withdrew their ambassadors from Qatar, but the eighteen-month feud concluded in an uneasy truce signed in December 2014. Importantly, however, the two sides failed to sort out the fundamental disagreements between them. Notably, Doha did not join the others in designating the Muslim Brotherhood as a terrorist organization and continued to host Brotherhood officials.

In mid-2017, the GCC hard-liners and Egypt again accused Qatar of supporting terrorist groups and maintaining cordial relations with their arch-enemy, Iran. At this point, they severed political, trade, and transport links with Doha and presented its government with thirteen demands that included shuttering Al Jazeera, closing the Turkish military base on its territory, halting support for the Muslim Brotherhood, and downgrading its nexus to Tehran. The underlying source of conflict, as a Qatari official observed, was that "we weren't going to become a [Saudi] proxy state" (*Reuters* 2020a). Saudi and Emirati saber rattling continued for a while – Riyadh even made plans to dig a canal to turn the Qatari peninsula into an island (Al-Hashemi 2019: 53) – but its intensity has gradually waned. Nonetheless, the feud had shaken the GCC to its very foundations.

Qatar refused to back down, and its experience has supported the argument that the longer a blockade is imposed, the better the afflicted country adjusts to it. Rather than cutting ties, Doha re-established full diplomatic relations with Iran. Though Qatar may have no illusions about Tehran's ambitions in the region, it must get along with it for a number of reasons: proximity, power imbalance, and commercial interests. Perhaps the most compelling incentive to maintain peaceable ties is the world's largest known gas field, discovered in 1971, the year of Qatari independence – the North Field for Qataris, South Pars for Iranians – the two countries share that renders a full break in relations imprudent, to say the least (Krane 2019b: 45). In late 2018, Qatar cut another link with its Gulf neighbors by leaving OPEC, in concert with its energy interests that privilege natural gas exports. Talks held in January 2020 to end the dispute faltered, although the boycotting states agreed to resume postal service to Qatar.

The conflict with Qatar has negatively impacted overall Gulf security. It has divided the GCC between the belligerents and the moderate members (Kuwait and Oman). Most importantly, the quarrel has backfired, as it has directly strengthened Tehran's position. Economists estimated in 2017 that if the crisis went on for a few years – as it has – then Tehran stood to gain "hundreds of millions of dollars in new revenue" (*Economist* 2017: 49). Iran is now less isolated in the region: not only has Doha upgraded relations with the ayatollahs, but neither Kuwait nor Oman has been willing to cut ties with them. For the GCC, the ongoing quarrel with Qatar signifies an existential crisis at best; it may well be the organization's final chapter.

3.3 Special Bonds: The Saudi Links to Bahrain and the UAE

Bahrain and Saudi Arabia have shared a special relationship ever since 1958 when their rulers settled their outstanding boundary issues (Wheatcroft 1995: 201). Bahrain is situated right in the middle of Saudi Arabia and Iran, two regional rivals. Saudi Arabia's Eastern Province, neighboring Bahrain, is also the kingdom's most strategically vulnerable, given that it is where its marginalized Shia Muslim minority live whose proportion is variously estimated at about 20 percent of the Saudi citizenry of roughly twenty-one million. The Eastern Province is also where the largest Saudi oil deposits are. Therefore, the political stability of and continued Al Khalifa rule in Bahrain, just across the strategically important King Fahd Causeway, is a prime foreign policy consideration for Riyadh.

For decades now, the Al Saud have treated Bahrain as a part of Saudi Arabia and have dominated its political and economic life. Bahraini living standards are kept at a reasonably high level, owing to Saudi subventions and direct and indirect subsidies to the island's economy. At the same time, for millions of Saudis, Bahrain serves as a "safety valve," a friendly state nearby where they can blow off some steam (with relatively liberal rules and access to alcohol and prostitutes). All major policy decisions made in Bahrain must be squared with the Saudis first.[3] Recognizing Riyadh's leverage over Manama, US policy makers desiring political change in Bahrain need to ask for Saudi support of their initiatives.

At the GCC's May 2012 meeting, Saudi Arabia and Bahrain even proposed a plan to form a closer political and military union. This initiative, too, had floundered on the other four members' opposition who saw it as another sign of Saudi domination. Such a merger would have allowed the Saudis to block potential compromises between the Manama regime and its Shia Muslim population, would have changed the sectarian balance and rendered the Bahraini Shia a minority in the unified state, and allowed Riyadh to station their troops permanently in Bahrain (Wehrey 2014: 100).

Saudi relations with the Emirates are much closer to a partnership – a nexus between two countries of more balanced weight. Although in the past the UAE, along with every other GCC state, had conflicts with Riyadh, the two governments have become closer particularly since MbS had become defense minister in 2015 and developed close relations with MbZ, Abu Dhabi's Crown Prince and de facto ruler. Since then, Saudi and Emirati forces have been principal allies in their war against the Houthi insurgents in Yemen.

Saudi-Emirati cooperation reached a new high in December 2017 when the Saudi-Emirati Cooperation Council was announced, portending the two states' growing distance from other GCC member states. The Council, chaired by MbS and MbZ, would "coordinate all military, political, economic, trade, and cultural fields as well as others, in the interests of the two countries" (*National* 2017). Mohammed bin Rashid, the Ruler of Dubai, contended that the new alliance confirmed "the paradigm shift in bilateral ties" between the two states (*National* 2017).

Even the Saudi-Emirati relationship, however, is occasionally fraught with tensions. Although their rulers habitually deny any loosening of their alliance, strains between them are apparent in several areas. The underlying cause of the discord is the UAE's pursuit of its narrower national interests, even if it means having to leave its Saudi partner behind. Unlike Riyadh, Abu Dhabi never entirely cut its ties and had always maintained back channels to Iran. But

---

[3] Interview with Western experts on Bahrain and three Bahraini politicians (Manama, December 2015).

nowhere are the cracks in the Saudi-Emirati relationship more discernable than in the war in Yemen. The two allies worked at cross purposes and backed some incompatible local forces: for instance, while Saudis supported Islamists in northern Yemen, the UAE focused on countering them in the south. In June 2019, the Emirates began to gradually withdraw their troops, recognizing that there was no end in sight in the war.

3.4 Relationship with Egypt and Israel

Few areas illustrate the conflicts and disagreements between GCC states like their nexus to key regional powers. Since the Arab Spring, Saudi Arabia, the Emirates, and Qatar have often worked at cross-purposes in Egypt and the Maghreb. In Egypt, Doha has supported the Muslim Brotherhood while Riyadh supported the Salafists. In Libya, Tunisia, and Syria, the Qataris backed different sides from the Saudis and the Emiratis (Wolf 2019). Qatar has since regularly excoriated the policies of Egyptian President Abdel Fattah al-Sisi on Al Jazeera. Cairo desperately needs Saudi and Emirati financial backing and has been mostly willing to support Riyadh and Abu Dhabi in their international endeavors. In the first 2.5 years after his coup d'etat (i.e., between July 2013 and December 2015), Sisi's regime received an estimated $25–41 billion in the forms of grants, soft loans, and oil and gas products from the Gulf (Sailer 2016: 7; Abul-Magd 2017: 224, 237). Between 2013 and 2020, Kuwait, Saudi Arabia, and the UAE extended to Cairo about $30 billion in aid. Al-Sisi appears to take Riyadh's largesse for granted: "In a recording leaked in 2015 ... the Egyptian president mocked the Gulf's wealth. He told an adviser to ask the Saudis for $10bn in financial aid, a request that was met with laughter. 'So what? They have money like rice,' Mr Sisi quipped in response" (*Economist* 2020).

Since then, Egypt has participated in innumerable military exercises – thirty of them in 2016 alone – with various Gulf partners (*Al Defaiya* 2017a). Moreover, notwithstanding much domestic protest, al-Sisi transferred two small uninhabited Egyptian Red Sea islands, Tiran and Sanafir, to Saudi Arabia (Barany 2019; Grimm 2019).

Nevertheless, Cairo's support of Riyadh is hardly automatic. Even though al-Sisi has made grandiose promises about "defending the Gulf" from Iran, and that "military intervention to protect the Gulf states is part of the Egyptian army's doctrine," these statements stemmed from the need to ensure the con-tinued flow of Gulf aid than realistic pledges (Mandour 2016). In fact, Egypt did not keep its promises, and its contribution to the Yemen campaign has been far below what its Gulf allies had expected. Moreover, on a number of other issues, such as the Syrian conflict, Cairo's stance has been closer to that of Moscow and Tehran than that of Riyadh.

The Gulf's relationship with Israel is even more complex. After decades of animosity, a rapprochement has begun soon after the 2011 Arab upheavals for four principal reasons. The first is the growing realization that Iran was the archenemy not just of Saudi Arabia and the UAE but also of Israel. Second, the failing of US Middle East policy – the Obama administration's nuclear deal with Iran and recognition that the Trump White House's support of its Gulf allies was not unconditional – further induced Gulf-Israeli enmity. Third, GCC members have also come to understand the benefits of détente with Israel lay not only in cooperation in the security and intelligence fields, but also in expanded ties to the only innovation economy in the region with potentially massive payoffs in the agricultural, medical, high-tech, and other areas of trade. Finally, for a younger generation of rulers, Israel's treatment of its Palestinian minority and its refusal to agree to the 2002 Arab Peace Initiative are no longer the deal-breaking obstacles to rapprochement they were for their elders (Barany forthcoming).

Nevertheless, sharp differences remain between the Gulf states – or, more aptly, their ruling families – on how to approach their relations with the Jewish state. Elderly rulers – Kuwait's Emir Sabah al-Jaber Al Sabah and Saudi Arabia's King Salman above all – are more troubled by Israeli-Palestinian relations than younger, more pragmatic ones. Moreover, King Salman, as the Custodian of the Two Holy Mosques is a leader of and has a responsibility to the entire Muslim world that inhibits the Kingdom's readiness to embrace rapid improvement in its ties with Israel. And, while the Gulf monarchies are family states with few restraints on their rulers' power, Kuwait is an exception in that it has an active legislature that influences its foreign-policy orientation.

Links between the UAE and Israel, however, have continued to quickly improve over the past several years. In August 2020, the UAE and Israel decided to establish formal diplomatic relations. (The Emirates were followed by Bahrain a month later.) According to terms of the US-facilitated compact, the Israeli government suspends its plans to annex parts of the West Bank – actually the project was already shelved owing to heated protests from foreign governments and international organizations – in return for normalized relations with the Gulf monarchies. For Israel, the agreement was a massive domestic and foreign policy win, but the gains on the Emirati side are less evident. Cooperation in military security and other fields will expand further, but Israeli Prime Minister Benyamin Netanyahu repeatedly reiterated that his annexation plans were merely postponed, not abandoned (Wolf 2020). Moreover, Netanyahu has not relaxed his opposition to American sales of

F-35 combat aircraft to the UAE – one of the Emirates' long-standing security objectives – as he is concerned about jeopardizing Israel's qualitative military superiority in the region (Schwartz 2020).

3.5 The Failure of Fostering Cooperation

The GCC was formed in large part to protect the Arabian monarchies from the virus of the 1979 Iranian Revolution across the Gulf. As a joint military organization, the GCC, by any reasonable standard, has been a failure. After two decades, one of the very few achievements of military cooperation in the GCC was the establishment of the first phase of joint air defense command and control system – it provides secure communication between the member states' military headquarters – in 2001 (Legrenzi 2011: 76). Still, forty years after its creation, even basic building blocks of a military alliance (e.g., a common security policy, integrated air defense, ability to operate in synergy) are absent from the group. Not only has there been no substantive defense cooperation between the member states; they have not even agreed upon the principles that would govern such cooperation. There has been no appreciable cooperation in weapons acquisition among the member states. In 2015, GCC armories contained "more than twenty different types of troop carriers, ten different types of tanks, and twenty-five different types of aircraft" (Alajmi 2015: 57).

There are many reasons why GCC members have been unable and unwilling to develop a regional organization that could enhance their security. Even though the Gulf states share many similarities, they sharply disagree on the magnitude of the danger Iran represents to them. Similarly, not all GCC members agreed about the threat represented by the Houthi insurgency in Yemen to Arabia. Most notably, Oman refused to join the Saudi-led coalition. In fact, the rulers in Doha and Muscat might well worry more about the actions of the impetuous Saudi Crown Prince than the threat the ayatollahs in Tehran pose to them. As Legrenzi noted, "At any given point in the life of the organization one or more of the smaller states is fearful of the Saudi hegemony that would result from implementing an effectively integrated defense policy" (2011: 77). Since the GCC is unable to resolve its own internal squabbles, it would be irrational to expect it to join together in concerted action against an outside adversary.

The underlying problem of the GCC is the lack of trust between member states. The Gulf's ruling families have no faith in one another, certainly not the sort of long-term, deep-seated confidence in each other's principles and intentions that is indispensable for enduring security cooperation. Each member state has preferred to pursue and strictly prioritize its own primary defense against external aggression through unilateral measures regardless of regional plans and programs. As a result, what analysts wrote twenty years ago – "The GCC pact appears to add little to the mutual defense capability of the organization" (Brown and Katzman 2001: 5) – remains true today. To satisfy their needs for external allies, each GCC state has privileged the establishment of bilateral relations with outside powers rather than allowing the GCC to develop region-wide links.

4 The Gulf Economies and the Burden of Defense Spending

After the British withdrawal from Arabia in 1971, the newly independent Gulf states, "owing to the richness of their resources combined with their military capability ... [had become] susceptible to a number of external dangers that render[ed] them extremely vulnerable" (Ayubi 1995: 281). With the growing sophistication of technology, the tools of war, as already observed by Adam Smith, had become increasingly expensive. The Gulf states compensated for their small populations and wide-open exposure by hiring mercenaries and purchasing massive amounts of armaments. By the 1970s and 1980s, nearly half of the world's arms trade went to the Arab world, much of it to the Gulf (Gaub and Stanley-Lockman 2017). Since then, GCC states have gained the dubious honor of spending, on a per capita basis, more than any other world region on weapons, breaking records along the way – for example, the largest weapons deal in history (the Al-Yamamah sales of aircraft from the UK to Saudi Arabia).

Even among authoritarian states, military regimes and monarchies have been shown to have the highest defense spending (Bove and Brauner 2016). Considering the lackluster performance of Gulf armies, the question of how effectively their military budgets have been used is inescapable. What did they get for their enormous expenditures? What has been the rationale behind their choice of vendors and the weapon systems they decided to purchase? More generally, how have the Gulf states' defense outlays influenced their armed forces' effectiveness?

4.1 Economic Wealth and Health in 2020

The GCC economies, true to their reputation, remain wealthy by global stand-ards, though there are considerable disparities between the three richer and the three lesser-endowed countries. In 2018 the per capita gross domestic product (GDP) in current US$ of all six Gulf states was well above the World Bank's "upper middle income" average of $9,205: Bahrain's was $24,050, Oman's was $16,415, Saudi Arabia's was $23,339, while that of Kuwait was $33,994, Qatar was $68,793, and the UAE was $43,005.[4] The corresponding figures, for comparative purposes, suggest that while Qatar was close to the United States ($62,794) and Singapore ($64,581), it was nowhere near the super-rich European mini-states of Liechtenstein ($165,028) and Monaco ($185,741). Oman's per capita GDP approximated that of Hungary ($16,162), while Bahrain and Saudi Arabia were closest to Portugal ($23,407). In terms of the Arab World (average $6,608), even the figure for Oman was far above that of all non-Gulf Arab states (e.g., Algeria $4,114, Egypt $2,519, Iraq $5,834, Jordan $4,241, Libya $7,241, Morocco $3,237, and Tunisia $3,447). In 2017, Iran's GDP, at $5,627, was similar to Iraq's.

It is important to note that the provided figures are per capita numbers for the entire population and thus considerably underestimate the living standards for GCC citizens who earn far more on average than migrant or expatriate workers who, in turn, comprise the large majority of the population, especially in the UAE (87.4 percent) and Qatar (87.3 percent). Table 1 provides basic demographic data that clearly show that the most prosperous Gulf states also have the largest proportion of expatriates in their population.

The CIA's World Factbook ranks the Gulf countries based on their GDP on a purchasing power parity basis (with world ranking out of 229 countries) in this way: second is Qatar with $124,500; thirteenth is the UAE at $67,700; fifteenth is Kuwait at $66,200; twenty-second is Saudi Arabia with $54,800; thirty-third is Bahrain at $48,500; and thirty-seventh is Oman with $45,200 (all 2017 data).[5] A more comprehensive picture – one that takes into consideration life expectancy, education, as well as gross national income (GNI) – can be gleaned from Table 2, which presents data from the United Nations Development Programme's Human Development Index. In this table, the six Arabian monarchies are complemented by the seventh state on the peninsula, the Republic of Yemen, which (as can be readily appreciated) is in a different league from its neighbors in every measured variable.

Different measures of economic wealth and health would impart more or less the same basic message: by global standards, all GCC states are very prosperous and, in the context of North Africa and the Middle East, all of them may be considered extremely affluent. The six Gulf countries account for about 60 percent of the Arab world's GDP but only about 6 percent of its population if foreign

---

[4] All data in this paragraph is from the World Bank (2018), available at https://data.worldbank.org /indicator/NY.GDP.PCAP.CD?locations=BH/, accessed on January 2, 2020. For more detailed economic statistics, see the IMF Regional Economic Outlook Appendix (2019): www.imf.org /~/media/Files/Publications/REO/MCD-CCA/2019/April/English/Statistical-Appendix.ashx? la=en, accessed on July 14, 2020.
[5] CIA, "The World Factbook," www.cia.gov/library/publications/the-world-factbook/rankorder/ 2004rank.html, accessed on January 2, 2020.

Table 1 GCC total population and percentage of nationals and expatriates

Country (date)	Total population	Nationals	Expatriates	% nationals	% expatriates
Bahrain (mid-2017)	1,501,116	677,506	823,610	45.1	54.9
Kuwait (November 2018)	4,640,415	1,398,952	3,241,463	30.1	69.8
Oman (November 2018)	4,656,133	2,606,585	2,049,548	56.0	44.0
Qatar (October 2018)	2,743,932	348,479	2,395,453	12.7	87.3
Saudi Arabia (mid-2018)	33,413,660	20,768,627	12,645,033	62.2	37.8
UAE (late 2016)	9,121,176	1,153,576	7,967,600	12.6	87.4
Total	56,076,432	26,953,725	29,122,707	48.1	51.9

Source: Gulf Labor Markets, Migration and Population Program, Gulf Research Center, https://gulfmigration.org/gcc-total-population-and-percentage-of-nationals-and-non-nationals-in-gcc-countries-national-statistics-2017–2018-with-numbers/, accessed on August 12, 2020.

Table 2 GCC countries and Yemen UNDP Human Development Index Rank, 2019

Rank	Country	HDI (value)	Life expectancy at birth	Mean years of schooling	GNI per capita ($)
35	UAE	0.866	77.8	11.0	66,912
36	Saudi Arabia	0.857	75.0	10.2	49,338
41	Qatar	0.848	80.1	9.7	110,489
45	Bahrain	0.838	77.2	9.4	40,399
47	Oman	0.834	77.6	9.7	37,039
57	Kuwait	0.808	75.4	7.3	71,164
177	Yemen	0.463	66.1	3.2	1,433

Source: UNDP 2019 Human Development Index Ranking, http://hdr.undp.org/en/con tent/2019-human-development-index-ranking; accessed on July 14, 2020.

workers are excluded (*Economist* 2018a). Four Gulf states – Kuwait, Qatar, Saudi Arabia, and the UAE – hold more than $2 trillion (i.e., more than a quarter) of the world's sovereign-wealth funds (*Economist* 2019c; Gray 2019: 16–18, 104–105).

The GCC countries' wealth, however, still overwhelmingly relies on the export of oil and gas, even after decades of putative efforts to diversify their economies. The growth of Gulf economies remains highly dependent on hydrocarbon production and cheap foreign labor. Nevertheless, oil prices dropped sharply in mid-2014 and, owing to saturated markets and unsteady demand, have been projected to stay low for several years followed by a gradual recovery (Bahgat 2016: 39–40). Therefore, as Karen Young has observed, "economic diversification is beginning to look like a game of survival of the fittest in the GCC" (Young 2019a). The decline in oil prices and the additional impact of the COVID-19 pandemic have dealt bitter blows to every Gulf economy, even if their preparations to deal with this distress has varied greatly. In light of these developments, their extravagant defense expenditures make even less economic sense. Still, rationality and prudence have seldom been guiding forces of Gulf military outlays, and one wonders if adjustments will be made in the near future.

Table 3 collects the break-even oil prices for the GCC countries in April 2020. The table shows both the fiscal break-even price (the price required to balance the budget) and the external break-even price (the price required to keep the current account at zero; Cahill 2020). On April 14, 2020, OPEC's price of a barrel of crude oil was $19.70. At that price, all of the GCC countries were losing money by wide margins. This picture brightens if we consider the

Table 3 GCC break-even oil prices 2020 ($ per barrel) (market price of October 15, 2020: $42.15)

GCC state	Fiscal break-even oil price	External break-even oil price
Bahrain	95.6	80.8
Kuwait	61.1	50.6
Oman	86.8	62.1
Qatar	39.9	37.6
Saudi Arabia	76.1	44.2
UAE	69.1	32.0

Source: Cahill 2020.

average dollar/barrel crude oil world price of the past several years (2014: 96.24; 2015: 50.75; 2016: 42.81; 2017: 52.81; 2018: 68.35; 2019: 61.41). Even these numbers, however, make it clear why some Gulf states have been pressed to accelerate their economic diversification efforts.

Again, it is important to make the distinction between the richer and poorer (relatively speaking, of course) Gulf states. The social bargain between the ruling families and their citizenry is based on the state's provision of comfortable living standards (supported by plentiful well-paid and low-effort public service jobs) and generous subventions of everything from utilities and health care to education and housing. The rich GCC states, though cutting back on some of these perquisites, can still afford to be munificent. For instance, there is no unemployment in Qatar, the largest global exporter of natural gas, where the state's Investment Authority holds $1 million in assets for each of the emirate's 300,000 citizens (*Economist* 2019c).

Table 4 offers basic data and suggest correlations between the prosperity and workforce participation of GCC countries and their citizens. Generally, the richer the countries the less attractive their citizens find not just employment in the armed forces but being employed at all. Significantly less than one-tenth of Qataris and Emiratis participate in their countries' labor force. The richer the country the higher the proportion of their working citizens in the public sector – which generally offers higher pay and perquisites and less demanding work performance (Gray 2019: 150–153).

The majority of employed citizens in the Gulf – more than 80 percent of Emiratis, Kuwaitis, and Qataris – work in the public sector. Especially in the rich Gulf states, many citizens view public sector jobs as just another entitlement, like free education and health care. In 2011, UAE's Crown Prince, responding to the instability in the region, "ordered that 6,000 unemployed

Table 4 Public and private sector workforce participation in the GCC countries (%)

Country	Nationals in the workforce*	Public sector employment 2016**	Private sector employment 2016 **	Public sector employment nationals ***	Public sector employment non-nationals ***	Private sector employment nationals***	Private sector employment non-nationals ***
Bahrain	25.2	36	64	34.0	1.6	66.0	83.1
Kuwait	17.1	79	21	84.2	5.2	15.8	67.7
Oman	20.1	46	54	45.0	2.0	55.0	82.0
Qatar	6.1	90	10	81.1	6.3	9.8	81.8
S. Arabia	44.0	66	34	44.7	0.8	55.3	74.4
UAE	7.1	93	7	83.2	7.2	8.2	75.0

Sources: * https://gulfmigration.org/percentage-of-nationals-and-non-nationals-in-employed-population-in-gcc-countries-national-statistics-latest-year-or-period-available/, various years 2009 to 2013; accessed on August 12, 2020.

** www.statista.com/statistics/944703/gcc-workforce-share-in-public-sector-by-country/, accessed on August 12, 2020.

*** https://gulfmigration.org/gcc-percentage-distribution-of-employed-national-and-non-national-populations-by-sector-of-employment-2017–2018/; accessed on October 18, 2020.

Emiratis immediately be found government jobs" in an already saturated public sector – more than 90 percent of working citizens are employed by the state – where salaries started between $6,800 and $9,500 per month (*Economist* 2018b). In the Emirates, as throughout Arabia, the government encourages citizens to take private-sector employment, where 76 percent of the jobs are held by expatriates, the vast majority of them from Asia (Naidu, Nyarko, Wang 2016: 1741). Few GCC citizens – with the exception of Omanis – are willing to work in low-paying jobs or in a blue-collar capacity.

Even if some of their military spending may be considered unwise, Kuwait, Qatar, and the UAE are prosperous enough to weather the consequences of questionable investments. They also have their own grand programs for economic diversification (i.e., Qatar National Vision 2030), whose actual progress has been, politely put, unhurried. Kuwait has identified the goal of attracting foreign direct investment (FDI) as the main avenue toward economic diversification. In order to succeed, the government must transform the country into a more business-friendly environment. In 2018, the World Bank ranked it ninety-sixth globally in this regard – little wonder that it lagged behind all other GCC states in FDI (Fingar 2018). Even the UAE, the Gulf leader of economic diversification, has a long way to go, with the non-oil segments of its revenue sources – tourism, financial services, real estate – dependent on foreign investment and sensitive to political risk. Moreover, there are large economic inequities between the extremely wealthy southern (Abu Dhabi, Dubai, Sharjah) and the more modestly endowed northern emirates (Ras Al Khaimah, Fujairah, Umm al Quwain, Ajman). Dubai is the widely acknowledged success story: lacking major hydrocarbon resources, it started to diversify even before independence, but it has benefited greatly from the UAE's federal structure – more specifically, from Abu Dhabi's deep pockets. "The UAE," as the Emirati political scientist Abdulkhaleq Abdulla notes, "is a bird that flies with two wings, Dubai and Abu Dhabi" (*Economist* 2018a: 10).

The poorer GCC states, however, have already been forced to tighten their belts. Bahrain's economic fortunes are directly tied to its closest ally, Saudi Arabia. In many respects, Bahrain is a subsidiary of Saudi Arabia, viewed by Riyadh "not as an independent nation state, but essentially as a Saudi archipelago province" (Bianco and Cafiero 2016). Although not a major oil producer – it has the rights to half of the revenue generated by the off-shore Abu Safah oil field, owned and operated by Saudi Arabia – Bahrain has significant refining capacity. Riyadh also supplies Bahraini refineries with crude oil at discounted prices, another way in which it directly subsidizes Manama's budget (Matthiesen 2013: 31). The Saudis, ever mindful of Bahrain's domestic and external security issues, nonetheless need to carefully adjust the flow of their subsidies to the tiny island kingdom. Even though Manama has faced more or less continuous popular unrest from its Shia Muslim majority and criticism from Sunni political activists since 1994, it has been forced to reconsider the provision of economic benefits to its citizens owing to nagging fiscal deficits. In 2013, for instance, Bahrain spent about one-third of its state budget (9 percent of its GDP) on food, fuel, and utility subsidies – clearly unsustainable at a time when public debt surpassed 50 percent of the GDP (in 2015; Abdulaal 2015; Krane 2019a).

In 2018, when deficit amounted to 12 percent of the GDP and oil still provided 70 percent of state income, the Manama government announced plans for the introduction of a value-added tax (VAT) in the following year, raised gas prices, and further reduced some endowments to its citizens. In the same year, Bahrain received $10 billion of aid over five years from Saudi Arabia, Kuwait, and the UAE, but given the state of its economy, this aid package amounted to little more than a stop-gap measure. In 2019 the country's fiscal deficit, according to the IMF, was 10.6 percent of its GDP, a figure that was expected to jump to 15.7 percent in 2020 (*Reuters* 2020b). Bahrain has already implemented some much-needed reforms and one wonders what room is realistically left to close the yawning gap between its spending and revenues.

Bahrain has been trying to move away from reliance on oil since the 1960s. Manama has established a thriving finance sector (a beneficiary of large-scale money transfers following the onset of the Lebanese civil war) and invested in tourism – though the former cannot compete with Dubai and the latter took a hit after the government's suppression of the 2011 uprising and well-publicized human rights violations. One important bright spot, especially in a GCC-wide comparison, is Bahrain's vibrant labor market: two-thirds of its workers are employed in the private sector (compare with under 10 percent in Kuwait) and unemployment, at 4 percent, is relatively low. These figures exclude security sector personnel and hence offer an incomplete picture. Bahrain has succeeded in creating a business-friendly environment that includes subsidized loans for enterprises and 100 percent foreign ownership of firms (*Economist* 2019b).

Since the share of oil sales in total government revenues in Saudi Arabia has averaged "well over 80%, and even 90% between 2010 and 2014," the collapse of oil prices in 2014 led to an extraordinary budget shortfall that amounted to nearly $100 billion in 2016 (Roll 2019:7). Oil revenues continue to constitute more than 80 percent of the Kingdom's income (*Economist* 2018a: 15). Since the break-even oil price for Saudi Arabia was $76 a barrel (in April 2020) and during the last five years the world market price, as reported previously, averaged far below that, Saudi budget deficits will continue unless funds can be made up elsewhere. The Iranian/Houthi drone attack in September 2019 that incapacitated a key Saudi oil refinery laid bare the Kingdom's economic vulnerability: it affected half of the country's oil output and led to a brief 20 percent surge in world oil prices.

The reforms spearheaded by Crown Prince Mohammad bin Salman within the framework of Saudi Vision 2030, launched in 2016, are purported to steer the Saudi economy away from volatile oil revenues. Although there is little doubt that this ambitious plan is more intensively pursued than the failed initiatives of the past, many experts have misgivings about the pragmatism and realism of the envisioned programs and their goals. For instance, the management of the reform package is highly centralized and dominated by government bureaucrats. Economists who disagree with the envisioned reforms soon find themselves without a job or worse. One who criticized the initial public offering (IPO) of Saudi Arabian Oil Company (Aramco) – the world's second-largest company, with a market capitalization of $1.76 trillion – faced terrorism charges (*Reuters* 2018a).

The hallmarks of Vision 2030 are "gigaprojects," those costing $10 billion or more, "familiarly grandiose, statist, potential white elephants that have little to do with indigenous Saudi economic development," and unrealistic time pressures that lead to frequent turnover of key personnel and confusion (Partrick 2019). Neom, the high-tech city on the Red Sea with an initial price tag of $500 billion, has thus far failed to attract the throngs of foreign investors Riyadh had hoped for due to lack of specifics and guarantees. More troubling from a politico-economic perspective but hardly surprising given the Crown Prince's history, the "implementation of Vision 2030 is bypassing state institutions, creating a public policy crisis, and further weakening government institutions" (Fathallah 2019). MbS, well aware of the global trend pivoting away from hydrocarbons, has accelerated work on his projects, notwithstanding the Saudi economy's IMF-expected contraction of 6.8 percent in 2020 (Kalin 2020).

The long-standing state subsidies for fuel, electricity, and water in Saudi Arabia, in an era of dwindling oil prices, have claimed a growing proportion of government spending. Energy subsidies in 2015 cost $61.5 billion, or 9.3 percent of the GDP (Bahgat 2016: 45–46; Krane 2019b: 116–135). The Kingdom imposed a new 5 percent VAT and taxes on tobacco and sweetened drinks, lowered fuel subventions, publicly floated the idea of introducing some form of income tax, and began to sell some state-owned firms. In 2019, the public offering of Saudi Aramco, after several delays and three years in preparation, raised only $26 billion – instead of the projected $150 billion – mostly from domestic investors, even though, to make the stock more appealing, a royal decree greatly reduced the company's tax burden (Roll 2019: 7). Partly as a result of annual deficits between $40 and $60 billion, Saudi Arabia's sovereign wealth fund has shrunk by 40 percent in the past several years and in late 2019 stood below $500 billion (Ellyatt 2019).

One of Saudi Arabia's biggest problems is its distorted labor market. With two-thirds of Saudi workers already in public-sector jobs – which pay about three times more than private-sector ones – "the state cannot afford to create more do-nothing jobs." Just to maintain the current 13 percent unemployment rate – among young people aged twenty to twenty-four, it is 38.8 percent – Riyadh must create a million positions in the private sector in 2018–2023, a wildly unrealistic number when considering that it managed less than half of that in the previous decade (2007–2016; *Economist* 2018a: 11). Furthermore, the private business sector has negative incentives to hire Saudi nationals who are less skilled and trained but are accustomed to working fewer hours and wanting more money than foreign workers.[6]

The Gulf economy in the most precarious state is Oman's that, after years of trying to diversify its economy, has struggled to wean its reliance off crude oil exports. In 2017, 16.9 percent of Omani citizens were unemployed (and more than 30 percent of young people), causing serious social and political tensions (Ennis and al-Jamali 2014; Obouzzohour 2020).

As a result, Oman, along with Saudi Arabia and Kuwait, has recently pursued an intensive program of reducing its foreign workforce. This is just one of the numerous sweeping measures that Muscat tries to implement – others include restructuring the bureaucracy, establishing a sovereign wealth fund, simplifying foreign investment laws to attract investors – in order to fundamentally reform its state and economy and prepare them for future challenges. The Omani Vision 2040 development plan – issued in 2017 as a repackaged version of the 1995 plan ("Vision 2020") – calls for investment in tourism, technology start-ups, establishing free industrial zones near the port cities of Salalah and Duqm, and boosting farm production. The chief targets of Vision 2040 are that 93 percent of economic activity be driven by non-oil sectors and 43 percent of Omanis be employed in the private sector (Batrawy, 2020).

Oman's oil and gas reserves are set to deplete in fourteen and twenty-seven years, respectively. Even recent advances in extraction techniques are unlikely to make sustained production financially viable. In recent years, petroleum and natural gas sales made up over 70 percent of government revenues. Muscat's experience with cutting back social provisions also shows its downside. In 2016, widening deficits led the Sultanate to reduce energy subsidies, but protests in early 2017 forced the government to reinstate somewhat diminished

---

[6] Interview with Yitzhak Gal, Dayan Center, Tel-Aviv University (October 26, 2017).

price supports (Assl 2018). Some of these policies began to bear results, as since 2016 budget deficits have shrunk (in 2017 it was $9.1 billion, or 10 percent of GDP; Dourian 2019). Oman must raise capital to finance its debt payments and fiscal shortfalls and, toward that end, in 2018 it has begun to sell off some state assets, including gas pipelines ($480 million) and a 10 percent stake in its Khazzan gas field ($1.3 billion) to Petronas, Malaysia's national oil company (Young 2019b).

4.2 Defense Budgets Prior to 2011

From the moment of their independence (Saudi Arabia 1932; Oman 1951; Kuwait, 1961; Bahrain, Qatar, and the UAE 1971), four of the latter Gulf states have been both rich and vulnerable to external security threats. One way to deter these threats was to build up formidable arsenals purchased from close allies, primarily the United States and Britain, but also from a wide variety of other countries. Consequently, defense spending in Arabia has been high by most standards. Even prior to the 1979 Iranian Revolution, military outlays in the Gulf had increased rapidly. Saudi Arabia, for instance, increased its defense expenditures between 1972 and 1977 by 62.1 percent, at a time when they grew by only 6.5 and 5.8 percent in the United States and the United Kingdom, respectively (Whynes 1979: 11). Increases in military outlays continued in the 1980s, then slightly diminished in the early 1990s, before they began to rise swiftly again toward the end of that decade. Saudi military expenditures, for instance, went from $26.5 in 1997 to $32 billion in 2001 (a 20.7 percent surge), while the UAE boosted its defense spending in the same four-year period by a whopping 66 percent (from $6 billion to $10 billion: Jarzabek 2016).

Between 1997 and 2009, the annual combined defense expenditures of the GCC states more than doubled (Cordesman 2010: 36; Hasbani 2006). In the last four years of this period, the US alone had sold nearly $37 billion worth of armaments to the Gulf nations (Cordesman, Shelala, and Mohamed 2014). Since 2007, the UAE has been second only to Saudi Arabia in acquiring American military hardware through the Foreign Military Sales Program. Table 5 well illustrates the major acceleration of defense spending since 2000, when one considers that of the more than $470 billion invested in US weapons in the Gulf countries in 1970–2014, only about $74 billion (constant dollars) was spent in the three decades between 1970 and 2000 and nearly $400 billion in the fourteen years thereafter.

Not surprisingly, the largest spender in the Gulf is Saudi Arabia, but all six Arabian monarchies devote far more resources on defense than most countries of similar size and economic prowess. In 1988–2005, Saudi military outlays on

Table 5 GCC weapons imports from the United
States, 1970–2014

Country	Amount (billion $)
Bahrain	3.267
Kuwait	36.252
Oman	27.830
Qatar	57.771
Saudi Arabia	263.986
United Arab Emirates	74.670
Total	473.775

Source: Anthony 2016: 29.

Table 6 Defense spending 2004 and 2010 in the GCC (in
$ million)

Country	2004	2010	Change%
Bahrain	677	915	35.15
Kuwait	5,500	5,000	–9.09
Oman	4,300	5,300	23.25
Qatar	1,300	2,100	61.53
UAE	10,500	18,500	80.95
Saudi Arabia	31,000	52,000	67.74

Source: Jarzabek 2016: 3.

average accounted for about 60 percent of the Gulf's (including Iran) total
defense spending. On a per capita basis, however, Kuwait spent far more
($2,729) than the UAE ($1,300) or Saudi Arabia ($934) in 2005 constant dollars
(Askar, Mohseni, and Daneshvar 2009: 40–41). In 1974–2006, Riyadh was the
world's fourth largest arms importer. Just how heavily weaponized the larger
Middle East region was is suggested by the rankings in the same period of Iraq
(third) and the Iran-Turkey-Egypt-Libya quartet (fifth to eighth, respectively;
Askar, Mohseni, and Daneshvar 2009: 35, 69). Between the overthrow of
Saddam Hussein's regime and the eve of the Arab upheavals, all GCC states,
with the exception of Kuwait, increased their defense spending, though none
more than the UAE, which did so by more than 80 percent (Table 6).

In the last few years prior to the Arab Spring upheavals (2008–2011), Saudi
defense expenditures showed significant growth reflected by $52.5 billion in
new arms agreements and taking delivery of $13 billion worth of new weapons
(Cordesman 2018).

4.3 Increasing Military Spending after the Arab Spring

In all GCC states, defense budgets dramatically rose following the Arab Spring, even though aside from the one major Shia-dominated uprising in Bahrain and ongoing protests in Saudi Arabia's Eastern Province, disturbances were minor (in Kuwait and Oman) or virtually nonexistent (in Qatar and the UAE; Barany 2013, Hanieh 2018: 59). This development has been, in large part, a reaction to four security concerns in Arabia in the second decade of the twentieth century: the threat of domestic upheaval (particularly in Bahrain and, to a lesser extent, Saudi Arabia); the deepening of mutual distrust and growing conflict between the GCC (and especially Saudi Arabia, the UAE, and Bahrain) and Iran; the discord between the same GCC states and Qatar; and the war in Yemen. It bears underscoring that (a) in terms of politico-security matters, Bahrain, for all intents and purposes, is a part of Saudi Arabia and (b) Kuwait and especially Oman – in stark contrast to Riyadh under Crown Prince Mohammed bin Salman's dominance – have been doing their best to avoid conflict. In fact, much of the blame for all three of the four conflicts may be laid at MbS's doorstep.

Saudi defense expenditures rose from $54 billion (2011) to $87 billion in (2017), notwithstanding a significant decrease in the world market price of oil, the government's main source of revenue. Adel Fakieh, Saudi Minister of Economy and Planning, noted that more than 25 percent (or more than $56 billion) of the Saudi government's 2016 budget was devoted to military-security services (*Reuters* 2019). By 2014, Saudi Arabia was the third in the world in terms of military outlays and had maintained that rank even in 2018 (the last year for which data are available). Such high defense spending, of course, is also reflected in GDP terms. No country spent more in the 2011–2017 period than Oman, by far the least prosperous GCC state, devoting more than 12 percent of its GDP to defense every year in 2014–2017 (see Tables 2 and 6). For comparison's sake, US defense spending in the same period hovered between 3 and 4 percent of its GDP. According to data from the Stockholm International Peace Research Institute (SIPRI), in 2016 Saudi Arabia had the fourth and in 2017 the third largest defense budget in the world ($69.4 billion) – the UAE was second in the entire Middle East and the sixteenth overall (SIPRI 2018: 2, 7). SIPRI's data (Table 7) suggest that among the countries with the ten largest defense outlays, Riyadh had by far the highest military burden as a share of its GDP both in 2009 and 2018, notwithstanding a –0.8 percent shift, nine years later.

Table 8, based on data from London's International Institute for Strategic Studies (IISS), suggests that Omani defense spending as a share of GDP was actually somewhat higher than Saudi Arabia's every year between 2012 and 2018, and in 2013 and 2014 significantly higher – presumably as a response to

Table 7 Top 10 countries with the highest military expenditure in 2018

Rank 2018	Rank 2017	Country	Mil. expenditure 2018 ($b)	Change 2009–2018 (%)	Mil. expend. as share of GDP 2018	Mil. expend. as share of GDP 2009	Share of world mil expend. 2018 (%)
1	1	United States	649	–17	3.2	4.6	36
2	2	China	[250]	83	[1.9]	[2.1]	[14]
3	3	Saudi Arabia	[67.6]	28	[8.8]	9.6	[3.7]
4	5	India	66.5	29	2.4	2.9	3.7
5	6	France	63.8	1.6	2.3	2.5	3.5
6	4	Russia	61.4	27	3.9	3.9	3.4
7	7	United Kingdom	50.0	–17	1.8	2.4	2.7
8	9	Germany	49.5	9	1.2	1.4	2.7
9	8	Japan	46.6	2.3	0.9	1.0	2.6
10	10	South Korea	43.1	28	2.6	2.7	2.4

Source: *SIPRI Yearbook 2019*, 194. [x]: numbers in brackets are SIPRI estimates.

Table 8 Military expenditures to GDP shares for the GCC states (2011–2018)

Countries	2011	2012	2013	2014	2015	2016	2017	2018
Bahrain	3.63%	3.84%	4.94%	3.90%	4.95%	4.77%	4.19%	3.76%
Kuwait	2.50%	2.64%	2.56%	2.70%	3.60%	5.17%	4.83%	4.26%
Oman	5.90%	8.40%	11.73%	11.95%	16.40%	13.72%	12.08%	10.95%
Qatar	2.00%	2.03%	2.15%	2.42%	2.84%	2.80%		
Saudi Arabia	8.12%	7.79%	7.98%	10.38%	12.90%	12.60%	11.20%	10.70%
UAE	2.72%	2.60%	3.46%	3.60%				
Iran	5.47%	4.59%	4.12%	3.82%	3.64%	3.86%	4.87%	4.55%

Source: The Military Balance Annual Reports 2011–2019, www.iiss.org/en/publications/military-s-balance, accessed on September 9, 2020.

the protests in the Sultanate in 2011. Although the UAE has not published data regarding its military outlays in the last several years, analysts believe that the amount would certainly place it somewhere in the world's top fifteen.

These trends are likely to be reversed owing to diminishing revenues from hydrocarbon exports. In much of North Africa and the Middle East, real change in defense spending from 2017 to 2018 has been mostly negative (Saudi Arabia and Bahrain registering a decrease of between 10 to 20 percent, while Kuwait and Oman a more modest 3 to 10 percent; IISS 2019: 325). According to SIPRI data, Saudi military spending fell by 6.5 percent in 2018 to $67.6 billion (SIPRI 2019a, 186).

The most remarkable point that emerges from Table 8 is that in the 2010s Oman, by far the poorest country in the GCC, has spent a larger proportion of its GDP on military security than other Arabian states. Another noteworthy fact is that Iran, the GCC's main adversary, has devoted proportionately less resources to defense in the same decade than most GCC states, and much less than Saudi Arabia and Bahrain (and presumably the UAE, which no longer makes its defense budget data public). Finally, by the end of the decade, the share of defense outlays as a proportion of GDP decreased in several GCC states, likely, again, as a response to plummeting revenues from hydrocarbon exports.

In the last decade, GCC countries have committed to major purchases of American arms. In 2008–2011, $5.8 billion (of the total of $13 billion) worth of the weapons delivered to Saudi Arabia originated in the United States, while in 2012–2015, America sold $10.5 billion of the weapons (of the total of $17.7 billion) purchased by the Kingdom (Cordesman 2018, 11). In 2009–2016, the GCC imported about $200 billion worth of American arms. Under Barack Obama's presidency, within a five-year period (October 2010 to November 2015), Saudi Arabia purchased $111 billion worth of American weapons (Blanchard 2016: 39).

In 2017 alone, the US Department of State approved arms agreements with Bahrain ($4 billion), Kuwait ($800 million), Qatar ($12 billion), and the UAE ($2 billion; Harb 2017: 50). The largest deal, however, was apparently reached with Saudi Arabia in May 2017. The total amount, $110 billion, was revealed with much hype by President Donald Trump in Riyadh, but the agreement does not commit the Saudis to actually procure these weapons, and it is at best doubtful that they will find the money for such a large purchase (Niarchos 2018: 35). As it turned out, there was no "deal" – just vague letters of interest (Riedel 2017a). Indeed, two years after the arms "agreement" was reached – that Anthony Cordesman has called "little more than speculative nonsense and empty political spin" – it had generated only $14 billion in confirmed purchases (Cordesman 2018: 11).

Table 9 GCC states among the 50 top recipients of arms in 2009–2013 and 2014–2018

State	2009–2013 rank	2014–2018 rank	2014–2018 share	Percentage change
Saudi Arabia	4	1	12%	192
UAE	5	7	3.7%	–5.8
Qatar	38	14	2%	225
Oman	43	18	1.6%	213
Kuwait	63	29	1%	348

Source: *SIPRI Yearbook 2019*, 248.

A comparison of the fifty largest recipients of major weapons in the world reveals that in the 2014–2018 period, two of them (Saudi Arabia – Riyadh supplanted India as the largest importer of armaments in the world – and the UAE) were in the top five, and five of the six GCC states (only Bahrain is missing) were in the top 30 (Bahgat 2017: 73). The data compiled in Table 9 also show the massive increases in defense allocations, with the lone exception of the UAE, which registered a small fall in its share of weapons acquisition.

These figures are unlikely to reveal the entirety of the GCC states' defense spending. For instance, military expenditure is only a portion of the total amount of Saudi defense outlays, which, as the Saudi budget statement for 2018 notes, is divided into the Security and Regional Administrations Sector (its budget includes allocations for new projects and expanding existing ones) as well as a Military Sector budget. Also, though the work IISS and SIPRI do is extremely valuable – their methodologies are reasonably consistent and offer fresh data annually – it is unclear how much their figures take into account such items as operations, maintenance, repair, and personnel costs (including training). In other words, one should exercise caution before accepting the Riyadh government's – or, for that matter, any other authoritarian government's – budget figures as the true extent of Saudi defense expenditures. One might argue that the only portion these figures more or less reliably capture is expenditure on imported arms.

One large-ticket item these budget figures do not reflect is the cost of hiring foreign contract soldiers (i.e., mercenaries).[7] Not surprisingly, the highest proportion of foreign contract soldiers serve in the Gulf's three richest states, Qatar (about 85 percent), the UAE (<80 percent), and Kuwait (<65 percent),

---

[7] This paragraph summarizes Barany 2020a.

where few young men have any economic incentive to sign up for enlisted positions. Conversely, Oman has the smallest number of contract soldiers, most of whom are British non-commissioned officers who work as training instructors and advisers seconded to the Sultan's Armed Forces. The vast majority of contract soldiers serving in the Gulf are Sunni Muslims from the Arab world and South Asia. From the former, GCC armies tend to hold Jordanian soldiers in the highest regard, owing to their solid training, professionalism, and discipline. Although solid data on the cost of mercenaries is difficult to obtain, the $529 million contract Reflex Responses (a successor to the notorious Blackwater company) received to beef up the Emirates' mercenary army has been widely reported (Mazzetti and Hager 2011).

For the less well-endowed states of Arabia especially, such high sums and GDP shares of defense spending obviously denote a burden on state resources that are possibly shifted from social programs and investments that could provide meaningful improvement in citizens' lives. For, despite the general overall and relative prosperity of the GCC states, there is considerable poverty among Bahraini, Omani, and Saudi nationals (i.e., outside of the millions of foreign workers holding low-skilled jobs whose economic conditions are vastly inferior to that of citizens). According to some estimates, as many as 20 percent of Saudis live under the poverty line, and there are pockets of poverty elsewhere in the Gulf (Al-Khamri 2019; Hassen and Al Bilali 2019; Boughanmi and Khan 2019). Their strategic partners, like the US, need to recognize that overspending on security threatens domestic stability; that is, not using the Gulf states, especially Saudi Arabia, as a cash cow for armaments sales would contribute to economic development and socio-political stability in the region (Cordesman 2018: 14). Judged by his words, President Trump disagrees. He revealed his mind-set about the Gulf in March 2018, when, pitching a $525 million weapon system to the Saudi Crown Prince at the White House, he commented, "That's peanuts for you." The prince chuckled. After all, it cost less than his yacht (*Economist* 2018a; Walsh and Schmitt 2018).

4.3.1 The Cost of the Yemen War for Saudi Arabia

By any measure, the ongoing war against the Houthis insurgents in Yemen (since March 2015) has been an expensive proposition for Riyadh. Estimates of the daily cost of the campaign have run as high as $200 million and between $5 billion and $6 billion per month (Riedel 2017b; Gengler 2020). Extrapolating from the more conservative of the latter figures, the Saudi government has spent $330 billion in the first 66 months of the conflict (up to September 2020). Unsurprisingly, the air war has been the priciest component of the conflict: consider that a single Patriot missile can cost $3 million to $5 million, depending on the model, and the bombs Saudi Arabia has been buying from Raytheon UK and BAE Systems do not come cheap either (Paveway bombs £22,000 apiece, Brimstone £105,00 apiece, Storm Shadow Cruise Missiles £790,000 each; Merat 2019). Riyadh also has to fund much of the bill for the Yemeni government in exile in Saudi Arabia and pay the thousands of mercenaries in its employ. The bottom line is that Saudi Arabia, eager to transform its economy, is laden with the unnecessary burden of an unwinnable war, the cost of which has already eaten up more money than it now has in its Sovereign Wealth Funds.

To add insult to injury, for Iran, the Houthis' main financial sponsor and the Saudis' archenemy, the war has been a relative bargain. At a cost of "maybe $10 million a month," the longer the war goes on, the better off Tehran is going to be (Gordon, Doran, and Alterman 2019: 22–23). In fact, one may wonder how could Riyadh's war in Yemen have worked out *more propitiously* than it has for Iran, with the Saudis being bogged down in a war of attrition that strains their resources and creates growing international ill will toward them. One scholar reckoned that Tehran received a limited return on its modest investment in Yemen (Juneau 2016). I disagree: for Iran, this war has been the proverbial gift that keeps on giving.

5 Armaments Acquisition: How, From Whom, and Why

If the previous section was mainly about "how much" the GCC states spent on defense, in this one the focus is from whom do they buy and for what reason.

5.1 A Lack of Oversight Encourages Corruption

By its very nature, defense-security spending is the most sensitive part of most governments' budgets. In democracies, parliaments' most significant authority vis-à-vis the armed forces is the preparation, enactment into law, and disbursement of the defense budget. Elected representatives in legislatures debate and vote on military outlays and then monitor their implementation. Even the budgets of democratic states tend to conceal portions of security sector spending – individual items may be accessible only to defense committee members – or offer a few figures that are not broken down and pose an insurmountable test to the would-be auditor (Barany 2012: 29–32).

The absolute monarchies of the Gulf need not observe such rules or operate under such restrictions.[8] Since, aside from the partial exception of Kuwait, there

---

[8] This section draws liberally from Barany 2020b.

are no authentic and/or effective popular legislatures in Arabia, there is essentially no oversight mechanisms that could constrain defense spending. The GCC governments' decision-making processes in this regard, as in many others, remain opaque. In general, the perfunctory and/or hand-picked assemblies of several Gulf monarchies may offer inputs into social, cultural, or even economic affairs, but they have neither the information nor the invitation to contribute their views on military-security matters. For instance, Bahrain's parliament – which does have a defense and security committee – is quite powerful on paper but enjoys no actual capacity to exercise oversight. Ordinarily, as Saudi Prince Alwaleed bin Talal once noted, defense-related projects are "highly secretive and subject to no ministry of finance oversight or controls" (Kulish and Kirkpatrick 2017). In the autocracies of the Gulf, whatever check there is on defense spending comes from the royal family that is the state. Thus an important feature of MbS's much-touted defense transformation "boils down to better cash control" in Saudi military affairs: "controlling money as a way to deepen both political control and domestic credibility is a hallmark of the present Saudi leadership" (Partrick 2018).

So how is Kuwait, with its semi-functional parliament, different from the other GCC states? The Kuwaiti National Assembly (NA) exercises a certain amount of oversight through its involvement in the budget process.[9] The NA might schedule a debate on a portion of the armed forces' budget, the so-called normal budget of the defense ministry. These allocations are earmarked for salaries and pensions, medical and education benefits, infrastructure maintenance and development, and similar purposes required for the day-to-day running of the armed forces. The other budget, however – one that sets aside funds for arms deals, unspecified security activities, undercover operations, and the like – is not transparent.[10] Importantly, for budgets to become official, they must be decreed by a law enacted by the National Assembly. (Needless to say, when the Emir suspends parliament – as he has repeatedly done – these procedures cannot be followed)

The process of arriving at the budget figures that the Kuwaiti National Assembly receives for discussion from the defense sector is quite similar to that in many democracies. Each of the three main executive-administrative elements of the defense establishment, the ministries of defense and interior, and the National Guard (NG) compile their requests independently. Within these organizations, there are separate committees, including one on armaments, that draw up their wish list and take that list to the Ministry of

---

[9] Interview with Ghanim Al-Najjar (Kuwait, December 14, 2016).

[10] Interview with a Kuwaiti defense expert (Kuwait, May 19, 2019).

Finance. Once an agreement is reached – following a debate between the two ministries and the NG on the one hand and finance ministry experts on the other – the "normal" defense budget goes to the NA's Budget Committee. If that body does not give its consent to the proposed budget, it must state its objections, and then the two ministries and the NG return to the drawing board and revise their proposal until an agreement is reached. After the budget committee approves the defense budget, it must pass muster with the Public Funds Committee – an entity created in 1992 to fight corruption – that reviews military deals, weapons agreements, and so forth, and if it does, the entire assembly votes on it.[11]

Arms sales, and security-related transactions more broadly, are ordinarily accompanied by little or no transparency. As such, they create optimal conditions for corruption, especially in political environments where there is limited oversight on the executive branch (Roeber 2005; Serra 2006; Barr and Serra 2010). In the absolute monarchies of the Gulf, where only members of the ruling family have the authority to condemn improprieties, weapons procurement has often gone hand in hand with large-scale corruption or, as one Transparency International expert has put it referring to Saudi Arabia, "theft on a grand scale" (Kulish and Kirkpatrick 2017).

The wide-ranging embezzlement in the defense sector has impaired the effectiveness of the GCC armies: when the princes pocket their "share" of the transactions, army units do not get what they are supposed to get. The lack of information on the accounting basics and the general absence of transparency of Gulf military-security companies also "makes it difficult to access the economic effectiveness of developing a defense technological and industrial base" (Gaub and Stanley-Lockman 2017: 10). Throughout Arabia, the practical upshot of widespread corruption associated with military affairs has been not just exaggerated armaments acquisition but also the notion that a lot of it simply "disappears" and has often found its way to the arsenals of ISIS, Al-Qaida, or the Houthis (*Economist* 2015; Farzanegan 2018).

The wide-ranging fraud related to armament procurement in the Gulf has been well documented. One of the most famous cases is connected to Prince Bandar bin Sultan, a former Saudi ambassador to Washington and a confidant of former president George W. Bush. Bandar, it was alleged, "bought an entire village in the Cotswolds, a picturesque area of central England, and a 2,000-acre sporting estate with part of the proceeds from kickbacks he received in the [aforementioned] al-Yamamah arms deal" with the British defense company

---

[11] Interviews with Ahmad Al-Sadoun, former Speaker of the National Assembly (1985–1999 and 2012; Kuwait, December 15, 2016) and Major General (Ret.) Abdulwahab Al-Roumi (Kuwait, May 22, 2019).

BAE (Hirst 2017; Wehring 2018: 169–177). Prince Miteb bin Abdullah, one of the MbS's hostages at Riyadh's Ritz-Carlton hostage in November 2017, had diverted billions of dollars from the National Guard he had commanded by "hiring ghost employees and paying inflated contracts to companies he owned for equipment like walkie-talkies and bulletproof military gear" (Kulish and Kirkpatrick 2017; *Guardian* 2017).

A more recent corruption scandal in Kuwait caused the removal/resignations of the prime minister and several cabinet members. At issue was the misman-agement of $790 million in the "Army Fund," a military welfare endowment that is used to give interest-free loans to uniformed officers of the armed forces. The Emir removed his son, Defense Minister, and Deputy Prime Minister (Nasser Sabah al-Ahmad al-Sabah) and the Interior Minister (Sheikh Khalid al-Jarrah al-Sabah) from their posts to let the investigation by the public prosecutor run its course. Prime Minister Jaber Al Mubarak Al Sabah, accused of failing to address repeated queries regarding financial irregularities, submitted his resig-nation and later was refused reappointment by the Emir. Even so, transparency was to be avoided, as indicated by the gag order put in place by the commission in charge of investigating public malfeasance by government ministers.[12] In the background of this turmoil is not only the spread of high-level fraud in Kuwait but also the jockeying for power and position in the ruling Al-Sabah family to succeed the non-agenarian Emir. In January 2020, the Kuwaiti justice system registered a first: the former Minister of Health, Ali Al Obeidi, was sentenced to seven years in prison on corruption charges (Al Sherbini 2020).

One of the common ways in which corruption occurs is that when defense manufacturers conclude deals with purchasing governments, they sign "offsets" (incentive contracts) to facilitate weapons sales. These generally signify "investments in the importing country's indigenous defense industry or some politically important commercial sector" (Marshall 2010). To be sure, there are financial penalties attached to misusing these arrangements, but at a US Congressional hearing, one industry leader professed to have never heard of anyone paying a fine. The absence "of transparency in arms imports and offset programs has also sometimes led to substantial corruption" and have indirectly contributed to the armed forces' ineffectiveness (Marshall 2010).

Are Gulf countries more corrupt than others with no public control over state finances? The well-regarded Transparency International has compiled an index that aims to measure the perception of corruption around the world. The data in Table 10 reveal that in global terms the GCC states are nowhere near the bottom of the corruption scale (Cordesman 2018: 5).

---

[12] Telephone interview with a Kuwaiti expert (November 23, 2019).

Table 10 Corruption Perception Index rankings

Country	2003 rank	2003 score	2008 rank	2008 score	2013 rank	2013 score	2018 rank	2018 score
Bahrain	27/133	6.1/10	43/180	5.4/10	57/177	48/100	99/180	36/100
Kuwait	35/133	5.3/10	65/180	4.3/10	69/177	43/100	78/180	41/100
Oman	26/133	6.3/10	41/180	5.5/10	61/177	47/100	53/180	52/100
Qatar	32/133	5.6/10	28/180	6.5/10	28/100	68/100	33/180	62/100
Saudi Arabia	46/133	4.5/10	80/180	3.5/10	63/177	46/100	58/180	49/100
UAE	37/133	5.2/10	35/180	5.9/10	26/177	69/100	23/180	70/100

Source: Transparency International (www.transparency.org), selected years.

Looking at the trend of corruption perception – displayed at five-year intervals since 2003 in Table 10 – shows some interesting developments that confirm the many stories and opinions one hears from citizens of various Gulf countries. Bahrain and Kuwait have been moving in the wrong direction (from 6.1/10 and 5.3/10 in 2003 to 36/100 and 41/100, respectively) while Oman, Qatar, and Saudi Arabia did not register unidirectional changes. For the entire period of 2003–2018, Oman has somewhat regressed, and Qatar and Saudi Arabia have slightly improved. One clearly positive story divulged by these data is that of the UAE, where surveys registered less corruption at each consecutive point in time. This outcome might reflect the Abu Dhabi government's growing attention to fiscal responsibility in the security sector, though an excellent recent research project concludes that Dubai remains one of the world centers of financial corruption (Page and Vittori 2020).

At a time when oil revenues are down, the desirability of fiscal prudence increases and the scourge of corruption becomes a more readily recognized issue. Saudi Arabia under MbS has pursued a selective and partial anti-corruption drive of sorts. One of the chief purposes of the November 2017 quarantining and extorting of more than five hundred extremely wealthy and well-connected people, most of whom were apparently the beneficiaries of fraudulent dealings, was to make the point that the new man at the helm was serious about corruption.[13] The Kingdom's Control and Anti-Corruption Authority – which briefs the Crown Prince monthly – has recently ramped up its activities; in the first half of 2020 alone, it initiated 218 criminal cases (Naar 2020). Even more remarkable was the dismissal of Prince Fahd bin Turki bin Abdulaziz, a senior member of the royal family and the commander of the coalition fighting in Yemen, over corruption charges in August 2020 – the investigation has focused on "suspicious financial transactions in the defense ministry" (*Middle East Eye* 2020).

As a result of regulations introduced under MbS, bidding processes have been revamped and major defense-related purchases now require the Ministry of Finance to sign off on them. Western firms have been asked to work with the Ministry of Defense in Riyadh to discourage corruption in procurement (Gaub and Stanley-Lockman 2017: 40). More generally, the paying of fines and fees has been simplified through the introduction of online apps to reduce unnecessary paperwork and the shame of court appearances (Partrick 2019). In the recent Kuwaiti corruption scandal, too, the emir took pains to assure his subjects that the government was taking corruption seriously and the law would be

---

[13] The detained group of individuals consisted entirely of people with whom MbS had a grudge. This point is also valid for those arrested in subsequent years (Kirkpatrick and Hubbard 2020).

applied equally to all (*Asharq Al-Awsat* 2019). Still, convincing people of the authenticity of these governments' newly found anti-corruption enthusiasm may not be easy. As one skeptical Western diplomat observed, "What is the law in Saudi Arabia? The law is the last thing the king said" (*Economist* 2018a: 11).

Cultural disparities are also at play when Westerners contemplate corruption in different socio-cultural settings. Corruption is perceived quite differently in the Gulf than in Western societies and business environments (Farooq and Brooks 2013). Those with extensive experience in GCC business dealings suggest that the modus operandi in Arabia has always been what Westerners call "corruption" – distributing tribal resources, making sure everybody gets his share, rewarding those who "make things happen" – but for Gulf Arabs, it is simply the cost of doing business, the way transactions are conducted.[14] No one expressed this more clearly than Prince Bandar who famously said, "If you tell me that building this whole country, and spending \$350 billion out of \$400 billion, that we have misused and got corrupted with \$50 billion, I'll tell you, yes. But I'll take that anytime" (Kulish and Kirkpatrick 2017). As a Saudi social scientist told me, "all those hundreds of princes must make money somehow so they buy lots of weapons and equipment where they can skim off the top. For them, transparency is a foreign concept: nobody is checking the books, perhaps there are no books."[15]

5.2 Who Do They Buy from and Why?

This section presents three main points. First, the United States has been and, for the foreseeable future may be expected to remain, the largest source of armaments for the Gulf. Second, much of the GCC states' weapons acquisition has been primarily motivated by political considerations and the desire to have prestigious, top-of-the-line equipment rather than the armaments their armed forces need to have in order to respond to or prepare for any real-world threats. Third, notwithstanding the stated reservations of some democracies about selling weapons to states with doubtful human rights records, those qualms are usually overridden by their economic interests.

Not only has Washington been the largest exporter of major arms in the world every year since 1991, but the gap between the United States and other leading exporters – Russia, France, Germany, China – has actually widened (SIPRI 2019a). In 2018, for the first time since 2002, US firms – Lockheed Martin, Boeing, Northrop Grumman, Raytheon, and General Dynamics – held the top-

---

[14] Interviews with Bahraini, Israeli, Kuwaiti, and Omani experts and businessmen in 2017–2019.
[15] Interview in Kuala Lumpur (May 23, 2016).

five spots among the world's top largest defense companies.[16] Although the United States has for long been the main source for Gulf weapons acquisition, its large-scale sales to the region started only in the late 1960s when American armament manufacturers became aware that the Middle East's conflicts were mainly fought with Soviet and French weapons (Niarchos 2018: 33). Subsequently, US arms sales to the region have grown steadily. American arms exports to the Middle East increased by 134 percent between the four-year periods of 2009–2013 and 2014–2018. By far the largest recipient of US armaments in the latter period was Saudi Arabia, which accounted for 22 percent of Washington's total arms exports (while the Middle East accounted for 52 percent). In fact, US weapons exports to Saudi Arabia grew by 474 percent between 2009–2013 and 2014–2018 (SIPRI 2019a: 231–234).

Though the United States continues to dominate the Gulf arms markets, GCC countries have been spreading their risks and hedging their bets: that is, they have widened their weapons procurement around a variety of vendors, most of them – though by no means all – American allies and Western democracies. The expansion of arms suppliers has, in a very real sense, allowed the Gulf states to maintain and increase their autonomy. They have used purchasing not only as a way of shoring up bilateral relations but also to make sure they have alternative sources of weapons: if relations with one country deteriorate, they will not be without supplies. If the US and West European vendors close the tap of arms owing to, for instance, their concerns about human rights violations, they can always turn to China or Russia, who are not troubled by such considerations. To be sure, switching to another supplier might signify extra costs owing to the likely incompatibility between new and extant weapons systems and potential contractual obligations. The key point, however, is that the emerging new elite command staff of the GCC armies – increasingly professional, Western educated, and knowledgeable of market conditions – also know how they can profit from playing the competition against one another (Hasbani 2006:81).

For example, the majority of the aircraft in Qatar's air force are French (Mirage and Rafale). Not surprisingly, though, in 2017 when Qatar needed to cement US support soon after Saudi Arabia, Bahrain, and the UAE began to isolate it, Doha quickly dispatched a delegation to Washington to purchase some thirty-six F-15 fighter jets (Des Roches 2017: 21; Coates Ulrichsen 214–216). That order is responsible for keeping Boeing's St. Louis, Missouri, plant busy until at least 2022. Saudi Arabia's aid of $3 billion to the Lebanese military to buy French arms in 2013 was widely interpreted as a warning to its American

---

[16] The top ten was rounded out by BAE Systems (British), Airbus (European), Leonardo (Italian), Almaz-Antey (Russian), and Thales (France). Chinese companies were excluded, owing to insufficient reliable data (SIPRI 2019b).

(and other) suppliers not to take Riyadh's procurement preferences for granted. Ironically, a little more than two years later, when Lebanon failed to condemn the attack on Saudi Arabia's embassy in Tehran, Riyadh scrapped the aid program (Hubbard 2016). Occasionally Gulf negotiators have been quite cunning – using thinly veiled threats that often work – in getting what they want from their American counterparts. For instance, there was no discussion of selling F-35 fighter jets to the UAE until the delegation from Abu Dhabi started to allude to their intention of buying fifth-generation Russian planes.[17]

Britain has also been a major arms supplier to the Gulf. In 2018 alone, it concluded agreements with Saudi Arabia for a variety of weapons sales and sold Qatar twenty-four Typhoon jets valued at almost $7 billion (Saudi Arabia already operated seventy-two Typhoon jets; Pérez-Peña 2018). The UK sold Oman, its traditional ally on the Arabian Peninsula, nearly $1.5 billion worth of military hardware between 2010 and 2015, including Hawk jet trainers and Typhoon aircraft (Merril 2016; *Al Defaiya* 2017d, Haieh 2018: 59–60). In 2017, Australia, eager to expand its defense exports, agreed to sell armaments to Saudi Arabia, while in 2018 the German government authorized further arms sales to Riyadh (four artillery positioning systems) and Doha (170 warheads and engines for Meteor air-to-air missiles: *Al Defaiya* 2017b, 2018b). In late 2017, Qatar's Emir and French President Emmanuel Macron signed a $14 billion deal that included the sale of twelve Dassault Rafale fighter jets (to bring Qatar's total holding to 36), with the option of purchasing 36 more as well as 490 VBCI armored vehicles, among other items (*Al Defaiya* 2017e).

As Table 11 demonstrates, GCC states have also purchased armaments from other non-US allies. Chinese weapon sales to the region go back to at least 1986 when Beijing agreed to sell Riyadh CSS2 intermediate-range ballistic missiles. The Reagan administration found out only a year later by when they were delivered and installed, causing a rift in US-Saudi relations (Riedel 2018: 93–94). Since then, China has worked hard to bolster its military-to-military ties with the Saudis and other Gulf states. In late 2019, Beijing was preparing to sell weaponized drones to Riyad – it had already been exporting aerial drones to Saudi Arabia, the UAE, and other Middle East countries (Wolverton 2019). China is eager to corner the Middle East drone market, as the United States, Russia, and thirty-three other governments are constrained by the Missile Technology Control Regime, an arms-control agreement Beijing did not sign (Economist 2019a; Tabrizi and Bronk 2018: 18–22). Recently, Riyadh has concluded defense-industry agreements with Russia as well (Al Defaiya

---

[17] Conversation with American security experts (Abu Dhabi, December 7, 2017).

2017c). Still, as Table 11 reveals, both China and Russia are currently only minor sources of weapons for Saudi Arabia and the Emirates.

In recent years, Saudi Arabia has concluded defense cooperation accords with Indonesia, India, Pakistan, and South Africa as well. The UAE has also purchased armaments from Canada, Indonesia, and Sweden. In 2017 the Emiratis explored the possibility of purchasing Russian Sukhoi Su-35 Flanker-E fighter jets but as of November 2019 did not commit to the deal (*TASS* 2017; *Defense News* 2019). Other East European countries, among them Ukraine, Poland, and Serbia – the latter signed a Euro 200 million agreement to develop cruise missiles with the UAE – have also become active in the GCC armaments market (Gaub and Stanley-Lockman 2017: 71). Oman has long endeavored to diversify its sources of armaments. In 2018, it further broadened its centuries-long commercial ties with India: Muscat reached arms deals with New Delhi and permitted the Indian Navy to use its fast-developing port facilities in Duqm (Castellier and Müller 2019). Although American weapons sales to Oman have grown, Washington has favored Saudi Arabia and the UAE "over unresolved border disputes between Abu Dhabi and Muscat, making access to Israeli surveillance and monitoring technologies an attractive backup" (Assl 2018: 3).

The procurement choices of GCC states frequently have little to do with achieving or maintaining combat readiness, let alone improving combined arms

Table 11 Top MENA recipients of arms and their top-ten suppliers (%), 2014–2018

Supplier/ Recipient (i)	1. Saudi Arabia	3. Egypt	5. Algeria	7. UAE	8. Iraq
China	0.7	0.4	13.0	2.2	0.3
France	4.3	37.0	0.4	10.0	–
Germany	1.8	6.1	10.0	2.4	0.6
Italy	1.3	0.1	4.8	2.2	3.2
Russia	–	30.0	66.0	1.5	33.0
Spain	2.3	2.6	–	–	0.6
Turkey	0.8	–	–	7.8	–
UAE	–	2.8	0.5	unavailable	–
United Kingdom	16.0	–	1.1	0.1	–
USA	68.0	19.0	0.4	64.0	47.0

i: Number next to recipient country's name indicates its world ranking as a recipient of foreign arms.
Source: SIPRI Yearbook 2019, 250.

or warfare capabilities. They often bear no relationship to pragmatism or cost-effectiveness, ignore budgetary trade-offs, and address no pressing need. Interoperability of armaments is seldom a consideration; it seems more important to have some fancy weapons that can be reported and shown off in *Jane's Defence Weekly*. New weapons are frequently purchased when the barely used ones break for poor or lacking maintenance or because the necessary tools required for their repair are missing (Heath 2016: 90). The acquisition of expensive equipment has often served no discernable rationale other than spending budgets or lining the facilitators' pockets. Instead of building effective forces through training and development, the wealthy Gulf states have been known to privilege what Cordesman has dubbed the "glitter factor" and "the shiniest toys for the boys" (2014: 50). In a recent study on Saudi defense spending, he concluded that the Kingdom's security decisions and investments over a period of decades have not been part of any coherent force improvement plan (Cordesman 2018: 5).

At the same time, as Emma Soubrier has argued, "the quest for state-of-the-art 'shiny' arsenals needs to be understood in relation to objectives of nation-building (making the population proud), state branding (attracting external partners), and deterrence" (Soubrier 2019). Acquiring such impressive armaments has also served the purpose of gaining international prestige and credibility (Soubrier 2016: 138). More generally, it should be recognized that, regardless of how dazzling, cost-effective, or necessary the weapons Gulf leaders buy, they first and foremost should be considered the indirect cost of the security guarantee, the premium on the security insurance. In a regional conflagration, the GCC cannot defend itself from the likes of Iraq or Iran. According to Stephanie Cronin, by the twenty-first century, Saudi Arabia had essentially "abandoned the goal of creating an army strong enough to defend its borders from external aggression" (Cronin 2014: 39). The many billions of dollars' worth of American and British weapons, training, bases, and so on help ensure that American and British soldiers will protect them if the need should arise.

The CSS2 (Dongfeng, intermediate-range ballistic) missiles Riyadh acquired in the 1980s from China were designed to carry nuclear warheads, but thus far, Saudi Arabia's desire to develop nuclear weapons has been held in check by American security guarantees. Still, there is a long-rumored secret understanding between Riyadh and Islamabad that in case of a critical threat to the Kingdom, Pakistan would furnish its nuclear weapons (Riedel 2018: 172, 176; Bahgat 2008). Government officials in Washington insist that Saudi Arabia is committed to the Nuclear Nonproliferation Treaty, even though MbS has stated that if Iran developed its own nuclear bomb, Riyadh would "follow suit as soon as possible" (Sanger and Broad 2018).[18] The first nuclear reactor in the Gulf was recently completed by a Korean firm in the UAE (about 140 miles from Abu Dhabi), while Saudi Arabia has plans to build sixteen reactors at a cost of up to $80 billion (Stanley and Lee 2018). Many American legislators, though apparently not the Trump administration, are concerned about MbS's nuclear ambitions, well aware that Russia's Rosatom nuclear power company is eager to build reactors in the Middle East (as it already has in Egypt and Jordan; Amlôt 2020).

5.3 Human Rights and Gulf Defense Trade

In democracies, presidents, prime ministers, and parliaments possess some influence over the flow of weapons to countries suspected of human rights violations, though in the end, business considerations often carry the day. For example, the US Congress blocked the sale of some high-ticket military equipment to Bahrain following its suppression of the 2011 uprising and to Saudi Arabia owing to its conduct of the war in Yemen. All the same, the Trump administration overturned these sanctions and many others. At the end of 2016, the United States halted the sale of precision-guided missiles (PGMs) to Saudi Arabia that used these weapons to destroy hospitals, schools, and other civilian facilities in Yemen. As Ted Lieu, a congressman from California and a former judge advocate general for the US Air Force, said, "These look like war crimes to me" (Niarchos 2018: 34). Trump, however, reversed the Obama administration's decision, and on his first foreign trip in 2017, he announced the renewed availability of PGMs to the Saudis.

Since then, his administration has routinely disregarded the advice of Foreign Service officers and legislators and circumvented Congress, declaring emergencies when there were none in order to facilitate sales of armaments and munitions to Saudi Arabia, the UAE, and others involved in the war against Houthi rebels in Yemen. In May 2019, for instance, Secretary of State Mike Pompeo pushed hard and successfully to allow US defense companies to sell $8.1 billion worth of munitions to the GCC combatants (*Congressional Research Service* 2020). In the summer of 2020, the members of Congress from both parties once again voted to stop arms sales to the Gulf countries fighting in Yemen, but the White House used its veto power to maintain the flow of arms to the region (Edmondson 2020).

The United States is not the only culprit: human rights activists, critical of Oman's record of quashing political dissent, have condemned the British government for expanding its military relations with that country after Defense Secretary Michael Fallon announced that the British military was

---

[18] For an excellent study of the larger issue, see Peterson 2018.

working "closer than ever" with Muscat and was exploring the options of establishing a permanent training facility in the Sultanate (Merrill 2016). More recently, the UK was again on the receiving end of an international outcry for agreeing to sell forty-eight advanced Typhoon fighter jets to the Saudis (Pérez-Peña 2018). In July 2020, the British government announced that it would resume the sale of weapons to Saudi Arabia because its review concluded that the Saudi airstrikes in Yemen that breached humanitarian law had been "isolated incidents" (Sabbagh 2020; Doward 2020).

The European Union's stance for human rights, particularly in the wake of Jamal Khashoggi's murder, has been somewhat more consistent. In October 2018, its parliament voted 321–1 to ban all arms exports "of surveillance systems and other dual-use items that may be used in Saudi Arabia for the purposes of repression" (Wright 2018). Holland halted armaments exports to the Saudis even earlier, and Sweden opted for not renegotiating a defense memorandum of understanding, owing to its concerns about women's rights in the Kingdom (*Reuters* 2016). In late 2018, several West European governments stopped weapons sales to Riyadh in response to the widespread famine it caused in Yemen (Stone 2018). Nevertheless, they, too, have been known to provide false or misleading data. A recent study by the Peace Research Institute Frankfurt concludes that Germany has for decades violated arms export regulations (Van Brunnersum 2020).

Canadian Prime Minister Justin Trudeau defended his government's decision to sell nine hundred armored vehicles to Saudi Arabia as one "in line with Canadian foreign and defense policies" (Kassan 2018). Needless to say, Russia, China, and other states unconstrained by qualms about human rights issues need not explain who they sell their weapons to and are eager to pick up the slack. Most probably, they are also little disturbed by the fact that their missiles and drones are far less accurate than American or British ones and, in the end, could cause more unintended death and destruction.

6 Arsenal

This section emphasizes the GCC states' recent armaments acquisitions, the issue of weapons maintenance, and the emerging indigenous defense industries in the UAE and Saudi Arabia.

6.1 The Gulf Armories

The GCC countries possess many of the most sophisticated weapons money can buy in the contemporary arms markets. If armaments manufacturers are willing to sell their wares to them, the Gulf states are likely to purchase them, often irrespective of any strategic need or rationale. The air forces tend to be the best kitted out branches of the GCC militaries – this is, after all, the service that operates the most prestigious weapons and where most of Arabia's many princes aspire to serve. Gulf navies have received relatively little attention; the naval capacity of even the UAE, Arabia's best-equipped and most effective military force, was mostly restricted to brown-water (i.e., riverine or littoral) capabilities as little as a decade ago.[19] The armies are generally well stocked with modern tanks, armored vehicles, and artillery pieces.

Whether the United States would sell its most advanced weapons to Arab countries – owing to Washington's primary alliance with Israel and its commitment to the Jewish state's qualitative military superiority in the Middle East – has been a serious consideration in recent decades. Here are three illustrative examples. In the late 1970s, Riyadh was keen to obtain sixty F-15 fighter jets for the Saudi Air Force, but President Jimmy Carter knew that the pro-Israel lobby in Congress was dead set against the Saudis acquiring such cutting-edge planes. In the end, Prince Bandar bin Sultan managed to convince the Israelis that Saudi Arabia would not deploy the aircraft at its airfield in Tabuk, near Israel (Riedel 2018: 60–61). In June 1981, the Israeli Air Force's F-15s and F16s flew over Saudi territory on their way to bomb the nuclear reactor outside Baghdad. The Saudis, confronted with such a clear proof of their vulnerability, requested US AWACS aircraft to enhance their air defenses – they are capable of detecting air and surface contacts over long distances – but the pro-Israel lobby once again objected. In the end, it came down to one senator, William Cohen of Maine (he became Secretary of Defense in President Bill Clinton's second-term cabinet in 1997), who changed his vote and paved the way for the sale (Riedel 2018: 87). Finally, in the early 1990s, the UAE wanted to buy advanced American F-16s, but US and Emirati officials were concerned that the Israelis would protest. In the end, after secret meetings between all sides – when disagreements between Israelis and Emiratis over the Palestinian issue and other matters were trumped by their shared perspective on the emerging Iranian threat – Prime Minister Yitzhak Rabin told Clinton administration representatives that Israel would not object to the sale (Entous 2018: 34).

Emirati military leaders have made the phasing out of mismatched equipment – dating from the time when the Dubai Defense Force still bought armaments different from the federal military – a priority and successfully persuaded Western governments to sell them their state-of-the-art weapons. When MbZ placed an order for eighty F-16E Desert Falcons in 2004, the UAE became one of Lockheed Martin's most treasured clients (Davidson 2008:

---

[19] Interviews with US and British naval officers (Abu Dhabi, December 2017).

265–266). Incidentally, for a time, the UAE Air Force had a more sophisticated fleet of F-16 fighter jets than the US Air Force. MbZ, insisting that he wanted the best, even offered to pay for the still-needed missing research for and development of a new radar-and-weapons system: he wore down his American negotiating partners and got what he wanted.

Since Gulf procurement has generally privileged purchases to expand air power, I concentrate on them here. All of the GCC air forces are well equipped with fighter jets, transport planes, and other aircraft, and receive new weapons regularly. Few, if any, air forces are better equipped than those of the Gulf states. Their expansion of defense expenditures in the wake of the Arab Spring has been reflected in the large-scale acquisition of new aircraft. In 2011–2013 alone, the UAE, for instance, purchased or placed an order for the following weapons: 25 F-16 Bloc 60 aircraft, a theatre missile-defense system (known as Terminal High Altitude Area Defense) with the associated AN/TYP-2 radar system, an undisclosed number of Predator XP unmanned surveillance aircraft, several multi-role Airbus A330-based multi-role tanker transports, 2 Bombardier patrol boats fitted with search radar and an electro-optical pod, and 750 Oshkosh Defense M-ATV mine-protected armored utility vehicles. Kuwait acquired 244 Patriot missiles ($308 million), while Qatar invested in an AN/FPS-132 Block 5 early warning radar (for $1.1 billion) and signed contracts for 62 Leopard 2A6 tanks and 24 PzH2000 self-propelled guns (all made in Germany). In 2012, Saudi Arabia signed an $11.4 billion contract for 84 new F-15SA fighter jets, Oman ordered 12 Typhoons, and both countries placed orders for Hawk trainer aircraft. Saudi Arabia also expressed interest in obtaining 30 fast inshore patrol vessels from the US, "reflecting renewed interest in littoral security."[20]

In 2017, the United States was preparing to begin talks with the Emiratis about the potential sale of as many as twenty-four of Lockheed Martin's new F-35 joint strike fighters, making the UAE the first Gulf state to fly them. In November 2019, however, the Pentagon announced that the current focus was on upgrading the UAE's F-16 fleet (Insinna 2019a). At the same time, the United States also approved the sale of ten CH-47 F Chinook cargo helicopters and related equipment to the Emiratis (*Defense Security Cooperation Agency* 2019). Few observers doubt though that the UAE will be the first Arab air force to fly the F-35s (and, other than the Israelis, perhaps the only one in the Middle East).[21] One senior US air force officer told me in 2018 that UAE pilots already flew more advanced F-16s – with more advanced radar, cockpit avionics, and double internal fuel range – than their American colleagues, owing to the fact

---

[20] Data from the entire paragraph come from *IISS Strategic Comments* (2013).
[21] Interview with a British military aviation expert (Abu Dhabi, April 2018).

that these upgrades were made after the US Air Force stopped buying F-16s.[22] The UAE has also complemented its fighter jet fleet with early-warning planes, such as the Swedish-built Saab Global Eye, which are able to provide ground, air, and maritime surveillance in a single package (Sprenger 2020).

Since 2017, Bahrain bought some used C-130 J transport planes from the UK, TOW missiles and patrol boats from the US, and expressed interest in acquiring nineteen new F-16 V fighters ($2.8 billion) and upgrading the twenty it already had (for about $1.1 billion; IISS 2019). Bahrain is the smallest state in the world to possess F-16s. In September 2019, its Crown Prince, Salman bin Hamad Al Khalifa, signed a deal to purchase the Kingdom's first Patriot missile battery (*Reuters* 2019). New external threats tend to further motivate new acquisitions. Within months of the beginning of the quarrel between Qatar and four Arab states in 2017, Doha, as noted previously, purchased F-15 and 12 Rafale fighters in addition to 24 Eurofighter Typhoon aircraft (Walsh 2017). Since then, Qatar added (some ordered, some already delivered) two An/AAQ-24(V)N Large Aircraft Infrared Countermeasure systems with related equipment ($86 million), Brimstone and Meteor Missiles, and Raytheon's Paveway IV laser-guided bombs (*Al Defaiya* 2019). In July 2019, Qatar was also the first foreign state to procure the US-made AMRAAM-Extended Range missiles to bolster its integrated air and missile defense capability (*Andolu* 2019).

For a group of affluent seafaring countries whose prosperity largely depends on safely shipping their oil and gas overseas, GCC states have paid astoundingly little attention to their navies. According to a US military officer serving in the Gulf, "Out of the three services here, sir, the navy ranks fourth in terms of priority" (Exum 2019). If they had spent only a fraction of the funds on naval force development than they have showered on fancy fighter jets, they might have the equipment to safeguard their shipping channels. One reason for this relative neglect may be that ships attract less attention and they are not as eye-catching as swanky fighter jets. Another reason is the Gulf states' reliance on American and to a lesser extent British and other western naval protection of their tankers. Some GCC military planners actually argue that the presence of the US Fifth Fleet (headquartered in Bahrain) in the region impedes the development of powerful armadas or makes it unnecessary.[23]

Though naval forces have long been the stepchildren of Gulf military establishments, Qatar, true to its maverick reputation, has recently begun to build up its navy. In 2016, the Emir appointed Khalid al-Attiyah, a former fighter pilot and minister of foreign affairs, as State Minister of Defense. Under al-Attiyah's

---

[22] Interview with a US Air Force colonel (Abu Dhabi, April 30, 2018).

[23] Interview with senior Emirati, Omani, and Saudi military officials and advisers (2012–2019).

watch – a period that has coincided with strained relations between Doha and its GCC neighbors, Saudi Arabia, the UAE, and Bahrain – the Qatari Emiri Navy (QEN) has embarked on an ambitious program. In 2017, Doha signed a 5 billion Euro deal with the Italian shipbuilder Fincantieri ordering seven vessels, including four corvettes, two offshore patrol boats, and one helicopter carrier landing platform dock. The deal includes a ten-year maintenance program as well. The QEN may also become the first in the GCC – and, aside from Iran, the only Arabian Gulf country – to operate submarines. Doha signed a new MoU with Fincantieri that covers the "supply of cutting-edge naval vessels and submarines" (Sutton 2020). The shallow waters of the Gulf favor light submarines, which Fincantieri has an excellent track record building.

In July 2019, Qatar opened the Al-Daayen Naval base in the country's northeast that will house the headquarters of its coast guard and will be a key element in regional cooperation (Younes 2019). The QEN also plans to open another new facility along with a new naval school by 2021 (Marchi 2019). The unavoidable question is who is going to sail Qatar's new warships and fly its new fighter jets. The QEN's current manpower is below 3,000 but it is expected to grow to 7,000 by 2025 (*Reuters* 2018b). Qatar has only slightly more than 300,000 citizens, and its armed forces have been staffed mostly by foreign contract soldiers (Barany 2020a). Undoubtedly, Doha will need to hire more contractors, while a sufficient number of citizen-sailors and airmen can be trained. Clearly, Qatar's quarrels with its fellow GCC members (2013–2014, 2017–) have partly motivated its interest in bolstering its defense capabilities. Improving the QEN's potential also aids the US Fifth Fleet in executing its mission, consistent with Doha's efforts, especially since 2017, to make itself a useful military ally to the United States (Roberts 2019: 8).

The arsenals of GCC states echo the configuration of their forces where the air force has received far more attention than the army – with the exception of elite and special forces – let alone the navy. Oman's military is the only one in Arabia without a clearly dominant service where the late Sultan Qaboos strove for a carefully balanced force.[24] The Sultan's Armed Forces are positioned around the country to render staging a coup exceedingly difficult and to respond to actual external contingencies: the army's 11th Brigade (headquartered in Salalah), for instance, is stationed near the Yemeni border.

6.2 Maintenance and Facilities

GCC political and military leaders insist on purchasing the most modern weapons but often lack the personnel to operate them. Some Gulf militaries –

---

[24] Interview with British military officers (Muscat, December 9, 2012).

especially air forces – do not have aviators with the requisite competence needed to fly their advanced aircraft. For instance, Qatar purchased its first two Boeing C-17 Globemaster III military transport aircraft in 2009 only to realize that there were no qualified military pilots to fly them: the air force had to borrow some pilots from Qatar Airlines who had the requisite qualifications.[25] Since then, Qatar increased its C-17 fleet to eight, having purchased two more in 2012 and another four in 2015 (Hoffman 2015).

Gulf militaries routinely fall far short of utilizing their top-of-the-line equipment optimally. In many cases, expensive high-tech equipment deteriorates because it is rarely used, often because personnel do not know or understand how to use it properly. Due to the poor distribution systems and logistics, the hoarding of equipment and tools is common – commanders conserve ammunition and spare parts as if there were no hope of resupply, with the result that those who need something most are the least likely to get it (De Atkine 2013).

I heard from a number of Western instructors one or another version of the same story describing the short-sighted and wasteful approach of Gulf militaries to equipment husbandry. Many millions of dollars' worth of shiny new weapons are purchased, briefly displayed and admired, and then put back in their boxes where they soon lose their luster because they are not used, not trained with, and not kept up.[26] One often hears from locals and foreign defense contractors (FDCs) alike, that, if need be, there is plenty of money to replace broken equipment – even if it could be easily repaired – with new, even more modern ones. The result is massive waste – the stories about the disused, rusting, or even uncounted and literally forgotten expensive armaments are legion – that diminishes the armed forces' effectiveness. As one American instructor who has for many years worked with Emirati forces recounted to me, "they have a lot of equipment they don't know they have, or how to use it effectively, or how to integrate it with other weapons. You give them pointers about acquisition, what to buy and what not: they generally don't listen and buy stuff they don't need."[27]

GCC armies pay infinitely more attention to procurement than to the upkeep of their acquired weapons. The state-of-the-art weapons that Gulf governments seem addicted to buying tend to be difficult to properly maintain. Aircraft that are not correctly serviced cannot fly the number of sorties they are designed to fly; tanks whose upkeep protocol is neglected break down. Because much of the

[25] Interview with a US Air Force colonel (Doha, December 9, 2012).

[26] Interviews with Gulf experts at National Defense University (Washington, DC, November 2012), and with British and American instructors and defense attachés (for instance, in Doha, December 2012; Manama, December 2012 and December 2015; Abu Dhabi, November 2016; Kuwait City, December 2016; and Muscat, May 2017).

[27] Interview (Abu Dhabi, April 30, 2018).

equipment in the Gulf is purchased for political rationale, there tends to be a large variety available that makes learning their appropriate maintenance all the more challenging (De Atkine 2013: 24).[28] Maintenance is rarely an exhilarating activity, and it requires a strong work ethic to do the boring things well, regularly, and on a set schedule. In highly professional armies, soldiers are trained to closely observe the maintenance schedules of their equipment – "Check it! Change it! Don't wait till it breaks!" – to ensure their reliability, extend their lifespan, and save money for the armed forces.

Several experts have argued that there is a "vast cultural gap" between Western and Arab maintenance and logistics systems and approaches. It is not just that "Arabs don't do maintenance," as I heard numerous FDCs remark,

> but something much deeper. The American concept of a weapons system does not convey easily. A weapons system brings with it specific maintenance and logistics procedures, policies, and even a philosophy, all of them based on U.S. culture, with its expectations of a certain educational level, sense of small unit responsibility, tool allocation, and doctrine. (De Atkine 2000: 21)

Not surprisingly, affluent Gulf Arabs do not want to work in entry-level positions, consider working with and dirtying one's hands demeaning, and want to avoid it. "Young Saudis are reluctant to work with their hands," and the discipline and constant learning of complex maintenance protocols appeal to few of them (*Economist* 2018c). As Kenneth Pollack explains, "[t]here is a consensus within the scholarly literature that Arab culture evinces a disdain" for technical work and manual labor (2019: 389). In the context of the Gulf, one might alternatively argue, though, that few prosperous young men anywhere like to engage in grubby and challenging physical work. In any event, many FDCs who work with GCC military personnel tasked with weapons upkeep and repairs tell similar stories of indiscipline, incompetence, and indolence (Heath 2016; Pollack 2019: 401–402).

Gulf militaries have resolved this dearth of willing and capable maintenance workers and technicians by hiring expatriate contractors to keep their weapons functional, to train personnel (generally third-country nationals, like Pakistanis or Yemenis) how to maintain them, and to provide logistical support (Cronin 2014; Heath 2016). In Saudi Arabia, there is a deep shortage of skilled mechanics and engineers, and in some cases even the right tools to maintain their aircraft. The Saudi authorities hire mostly American FDCs for a two- or three-year period – during which one of their responsibilities is to train local personnel – but, more often than not, they end up staying longer because their charges do not succeed in acquiring the needed competence. Arms sales often include not just the weapons

---

[28] Conversations with US and British military sales experts (London, March 2017; Washington, September 2018).

in question but maintenance and service contracts, especially if the purchaser does not have the personnel or the infrastructure to guarantee upkeep.

Maintaining sophisticated fighter jets is expensive. For instance, the 2016 maintenance contract for the Royal Saudi Air Force's 230 F-15 jets alone was worth $2.5 billion (Niarchos 2018: 33). The following year, the Saudis placed a blanket order training program at the estimated cost of $750 million inside and outside the Kingdom that included flight training, technical training, professional military education, specialized training, mobile training teams, and English language training. Many of these US contractors have reported a total absence of hands-on program management, "lack of discipline due to tribal hierarchy," and missing top-down authority from the commanders to encourage enlisted soldiers and officers to effectively learn how to maintain the aircraft themselves (Heath 2016: 90–92).

The GCC armies generally possess modern and extensive military facilities and infrastructure. They are constantly being expanded and updated because new weapons often require different accommodations (runways, hangars, docks, piers, etc.), and many contracts include language about the provision of new services and so forth. Another reason for the ceaseless building is that construction has been one of the most lucrative and corruption-ridden economic sectors in the Gulf and elsewhere (Davids 2013). Even in the last decade, a number of major projects have been completed or existing facilities expanded. For instance, the Jebel Ali deep-water port off the coast of Dubai – opened in 1979 to expand Dubai's entrepôt future – is the US Navy's most frequently visited port of call and the only one in the Gulf to berth aircraft careers (Ibish 2017: 23). It has served as a model for other deep-water facilities around the world (such as the Deepwater Port of Posorja in Ecuador). The Emiratis are also building military facilities abroad, including ports in the breakaway regions of Puntland and Somaliland in East Africa – although experts say that the military utility of these projects is highly questionable (Cannon and Rossiter 2017). In 2019, Qatar opened a massive coast guard base eighteen miles from Doha on the country's eastern coast that includes a modern seaport as well as training and medical facilities (*AFP* 2019). Qatar is also building a new airfield as well as expanding the existing Al Udeid airbase, home to ten thousand US troops (*Qatar News Ag*ency 2018). The Bahrain Defense Forces have recently constructed a large base in the northern part of Sitra Island and built a military hospital in West Riffa (*Gulf News* 2015).

6.3 Indigenous Defense Industry

Although the Gulf states have made some attempts at developing their own defense industries as early as the 1960s, these efforts did not begin in earnest until early in the twenty-first century. At that point, the governments in Saudi Arabia and the UAE allocated resources and drew up some plans in order to wean themselves off their near-total reliance on foreign weapons and military supplies (as late as 2006, it was still 99 percent [Marshall 2016: 249; Borchert 2018]). Needless to say, a homegrown defense industry would create jobs for locals, contribute to economic diversification, produce goods for export, and enhance the high-tech sector in their economies. To date, only two Gulf states, Saudi Arabia and the UAE, have been serious about developing their defense industries. Looking at their plans and efforts comparatively also suggests why, in a broader sense, the UAE has been more successful in transforming its defense sector than its larger neighbor.

In both countries, the rulers appointed capable and trusted people to head defense industry conglomerates, indicating their determination to see the project succeed. The potentially lucrative nature of building up an indigenous defense manufacturing capacity attracted a number of royal family members and high-ranking military officers to the industry in both countries. In the UAE, retired military officers have often served as front men, representing members of the ruling family. In Saudi Arabia, especially, senior active-duty officers have been involved in a number of corruption scandals related to weapons sales, with princes often lurking in the background of the deals (Marshall 2016: 254–255). Although ordinary GCC officers are not involved in the national economy like their colleagues in Algeria, Egypt, and Pakistan, some generals in Gulf countries have certainly not been immune to the temptation of bribes in the defense business sector (Porter 2019; Kuimova 2020; Giunchi 2014).

While the governments in Riyadh and Abu Dhabi intensively seek private and foreign investment, they have provided much of the financing for the development of new weapons with foreign partners. For instance, the UAE partially underwrote the research and development for Russia's most advanced anti-aircraft system and for GEC Marconi's al-Hakim missiles. These and other investments produced returns not just in the form of enhancing the country's defense electronics industry but also in actual profits (Marshall 2016: 255). Aside from financing large-scale projects, the Saudi government also offers loans for specialized companies, though the program has been criticized as being overly risk averse (CB Insights 2017; Ashri 2019). Already in 2013, the Saudi defense ministry passed a new law according to which domestic producers had to be given priority over foreign firms (Gaub and Stanley-Lockman 2017: 41).

As a result of growing opportunities, a number of defense companies were formed – especially in the UAE – and both countries established conglomerates to integrate and streamline business processes. In December 2014, the UAE

launched the Emirates Defense Industries Company (EDIC) with eleven subsidiaries that later grew to sixteen: they include both defense services and
manufacturing (firearms, munitions, aviation components). In
November 2015, EDIC had 10,000 employees, though there was no publicly
available data on how many of them were Emiratis (Gaub and Stanley-Lockman
2017: 48). In November 2019, MbZ announced the formation of an even more
comprehensive defense and technology government-owned conglomerate,
EDGE, that absorbed EDIC, consolidated 25 subsidiaries and employed more
than 12,000 individuals (again, it is unclear how many of them are Emirati
citizens; Helou 2019a). It would be a mistake to see EDGE itself as an indication
of growing defense industry ambition – its main objective is to bring about
stricter management of projects and to make sure that unprofitable firms are
weaned off government support.

Saudi Arabia inaugurated its own state-owned holding company, Saudi
Arabian Military Industries (SAMI), in May 2017 and, within two years, signed
more than twenty-five agreements with foreign partners to acquire alternative
technologies allowing the Saudis – subjected to arms embargoes owing to its
war in Yemen – to have a Plan B for product development and weapon system
projects (Helou 2020). The General Authority for Military Industries (GAMI),
established three months later by the Saudi Council of Ministers, is, according
to its homepage, the "regulator, enabler, and licensor" of the Kingdom's military
industry and charged with the building of a sustainable domestic defense
sector.[29] In November 2019, GAMI announced that it planned to increase
support for scientific research to 4 percent of the military's budget for the
next ten years in order to "convey technology, weapons industry, and military
industries in general" (Al-Sulami 2019). Aside from collaborative ventures, the
Saudis have been developing their own technology: some forty engineers (of
unspecified nationality) have been working on short-range ballistic missiles and
laser-guided bombs at the King Abdulaziz City for Science and Technology, one
of the government's R&D branches (Al-Omran and Hollinger 2018).

Perhaps the key difference between the two countries' conception of their
budding defense industries is the disparity in their expectations and ambitions.
In 2017 SAMI's chief executive, Andreas Schwer, announced that his company's goal was to become one of the top twenty-five military companies in the
world. He added that "SAMI aims to contribute SR14 billion ($3.73 billion)
directly to Saudi Arabia's GDP, increase the value of national exports by around
SR5 billion, invest over SR6 billion for research and development, and create
over 40,000 direct jobs locally by 2030" (Khan 2017) The Crown Prince is

---

[29] See www.gami.gov.sa/en

determined "to build a defense industry at breakneck speed" and wants half of Saudi weapons procurement to be done domestically by 2030, from about 2 percent in 2018 (Carey 2018). It is widely believed that, as so many of MbS's other programs and policies, these ambitions – that is, the localization of defense expenditures from 2 to 50 percent in 12 years – are "somewhat unaligned with reality," as two analysts politely put it (Gaub and Stanley-Lockman 2017: 40). The acquisition of imported large-ticket items – aircraft, naval vessels, tanks, and so forth – are inherently political and are made by top decision makers (i.e., the king/crown prince). But lower-end procurement – trucks, artillery shells, radios – is decided at the service level, and it is highly questionable whether or not the Saudi military would want to purchase local products instead of proven quality off-the-shelf imports.

Rick Edwards, a top Lockheed Martin executive, noted that "we support the Vision 2030 goals completely, but you are not going to go from 2% to 50% in a few years" (Al-Omran and Hollinger 2018). Cordesman is even more emphatic, calling the notion to develop the Kingdom's own defense industrial base "the silliest and least convincing aspect of the Saudi 2030 plan." He adds that there is

> virtually no way to waste money more effectively than trying to create an effective technology base or fund a weapons assembly effort in an area of industry and technology which is so demanding, offers so few real-world benefits in job creation, and where there often is so little ability to use the technology needed for specific weapons or purposes – particularly civil ones. (Cordesman 2018: 12)

In stark contrast, the UAE has been pursuing a mostly pragmatic program. Its target is to grow domestic defense manufacturing from 10 to 30 percent between 2015 and 2030. This, too, is a rather lofty goal, but considering that the Emirates already possess a more developed defense industry and a considerably more diversified economy than Saudi Arabia, it is more realistic. Rather than chasing vanity projects with little payoff, "the UAE arms industry appears to be focusing on developing 'good enough' solutions that can be mastered by the UAE armed forces and may have wider appeal on foreign markets" (Stanley-Lockman 2017). The Emiratis are driven to develop specific skills that would put their companies on the global market for niche commodities such as naval ships, advanced unmanned vehicles, and so forth (Samaan 2019).

Still, for *any* country, entry into the highly competitive world arms market, full of mature and experienced producers, is a profoundly difficult and risky proposition. For indigenous defense industries to be able to stand on their own without major state subsidies, they need, at the very least, a highly skilled labor force, enormous financial resources, and (often niche) products that possess a qualitative or price advantage over rival producers. Few small countries aside from Sweden and Israel – with far better starting-out conditions than the UAE, let alone Saudi Arabia – have been able to succeed in this market.

For the UAE, especially, developing its indigenous defense has paid some dividends. Since 2007, the Emiratis have been manufacturing the "Nimr" ("tiger," in Arabic) multi-purpose all-terrain armored carriers, co-developed with Russia's GAZ automotive manufacturer. The vehicles are produced at the Tawazun Industrial Park in Abu Dhabi. The company has developed a family of light- and medium-weight armored cars. The armored car market, however, is saturated and the UAE has no comparative advantage in that arena. In fact, this market became even more crowded with GAMI's mid-2020 announcement to locally manufacture "Ad-Dahna" armored multi-tasking four-wheel-drive vehicles for the Saudi security forces (Salama 2020). Tawazun has won a contract to supply 1,765 armored cars to the UAE army and, in 2012, reached an agreement to produce them in a joint venture in Algeria for the North African market (*Khaleej Times* 2012). What really happened, though, was that the Emirati troops did not want the Nimr – given its inferiority to the Western armored cars already in their arsenal – and the UAE essentially gifted them to Algeria. Experts believe that, for job creation purposes, the UAE would be far better off concentrating on operations, maintenance, and repair services.[30]

The Emirati defense electronics industry has grown both in output and sophistication as a result of partnering with top foreign companies like Raytheon. The UAE defense industrial sector has also acquired or made major investments in foreign firms such as the Italian Piaggio Aerospace and the Russian Helicopter subsidiary VR-Technology, managing to export its products to Russia and Saudi Arabia, among others. The Ministry of Defense in Abu Dhabi also purchased the first locally produced aircraft, Calidus's B-250 light attack aircraft (Insinna 2019b). Incidentally, the war in Yemen has served as a testing ground for Emirati-made munitions and armored personal carriers. By 2014–2018, the UAE became the eighteenth largest arms exporter in the world, ahead of Australia, South Africa, and Brazil: the top-three recipients of its weapons and security assistance (with their share of the Emirates' total defense exports) were Egypt (41 percent), Jordan (10 percent), and Yemen (7.6 percent; SIPRI 2019: 236).

Clearly, the UAE and Saudi Arabia need partners in order to build up a major defense industry pretty much from scratch, and American companies – many with decades-long ties to their ministries of defense – are well positioned to

---

[30] Email correspondence with UAE-based defense industry experts (June 5 and July 31, 2020).

capitalize on new opportunities of cooperation, licensing, and technology sales. But Americans might be disappointed. Both Gulf states have been open to defense cooperation with a wide variety of partners from around the world, some time-honored Western and Russian ones but also with some others – like Italian, Serbian, and Ukrainian firms – that are capital poor and hope to reverse their fortunes through an infusion of money from the Gulf. Turkey and Russia, with their own established arms industries, are eager to convert their growing influence in the region into tangible business gains. The competition in the world arms markets is fierce as more, and more countries realize the great profit potential in weapons production and sales. While Abu Dhabi and Riyadh might give some of its defense business to other producers, America is likely to supply the lion's share of its arms for the foreseeable future.

Much of the world's armament business is conducted at huge security-related exhibitions, and the UAE and Saudi Arabia have been hosting the most lavishly presented ones for more than a decade now. These trade shows usually attract hundreds of vendors and tens of thousands of visitors, who display their shiny wares (not unlike international car shows) with much fanfare. For instance, the Armed Forces Exhibition for Diversity of Requirements & Capabilities (AFED 18) in Riyadh in February–March 2018 – organized by the Saudi Ministry of Defense – brought together more than fifty international companies, with fully attended seminars and workshops showcasing Saudi weapons and targeting cooperative ventures. Saudi Major General Attiya Al-Maliki said that while the Kingdom had organized these trade shows annually since 2010, the turning point was 2016 when local companies first presented competitive products (*Al Defaiya* 2018a).

At the November 2019 Dubai Airshow – one of the world's largest, with 1,288 exhibitors and 161 aircraft on display – EDGE occupied the biggest pavilion to showcase the capabilities of its subsidiaries. The five-day event attracted more than 84,000 attendees; "sales were also booming, with the order book on site reaching $54.5 billion by close of business."[31] In July 2020, GAMI announced the launch of a bi-annual "World Defense Show," starting in 2022. It will feature the "latest innovations in interoperability across air, land, sea, security, and satellite defense systems," and as such, it is intended to be "the first truly integrated defense show" (Saudi-US Trade Group 2020).

7 Conclusion

An army's effectiveness and material endowments are separate though related matters and, as history has shown over and over again, a "poorly endowed military can be highly effective if it uses its resources well" and a "wealthy

---

[31] www.dubaiairshow.aero, accessed on September 6, 2020.

military can be extremely ineffective if it wastes them" (Brooks 2003: 154). In spite of the enormous sums Gulf countries have spent on defense, the gap between their armaments and actual capabilities to deter aggression and to defend themselves has narrowed but little since their incompetent performances in the 1990s (Bahgat 1995: 61). In other words, just how well have Gulf militaries utilized the hundreds of billions of dollars their governments have devoted to their defense-security sectors is, at best, highly questionable. An important reason for this conclusion is that there is essentially no oversight over defense expenditures in the GCC. This is a particularly important issue when considering the major burden military expenditures have signified, particularly on the economies of the less well-endowed Gulf monarchies. The wrong weapons, large-scale waste, widespread corruption, and lacking oversight all sap the effectiveness of Arabia's armies.

The Saudi military's poor performance in the Yemen War has starkly illustrated several problems rooted in the adverse phenomena mentioned earlier. Clearly, the Saudi armed forces' equipment was inappropriate for the challenges they faced on the battlefield or its personnel did not know how to exploit their capabilities. For instance, the Patriot surface-to-air missile system employed by the Saudis uses the AN/MPQ-53/65 radar, with a field view of 120°, but failed to intercept a number of missiles and UAVs (unmanned aerial vehicles) launched by the enemy mainly because it was set up and positioned incorrectly (Binnie 2019). They could not take advantage of more than three hundred ultra-sophisticated Abrams tanks (of which they lost at least twenty in the first sixteen months of the war; Weisgerber 2016) and forty-eight French-made Caesar self-propelled Howitzer guns either, as they were unsuited to the difficult terrain of north Yemeni weapons (McDowall, Stewart, and Rhode, 2016).

If one considers the sheer quantity of state-of-the-art weapons GCC states have highlands. Even some Saudi analysts admitted that their army's performance had been "patchy and varied greatly from unit to unit" and was hampered by their lack of battlefield surveillance technology – technology that is, of course, readily available in arms markets but does not carry the cachet of "more sparkly" acquired, then Arabia is clearly a heavily militarized region, but it is not one well protected by its own armed forces. Arms purchases in the Gulf have been more frequently prompted by political reasons and vanity than carefully thought out strategic plans. Arabia's armies are "long on hardware [but] short on power"; their arsenals are "too often for show and not for waging modern warfare" (Russell 2009: 35–40). They need to start developing armories with weapons suited to their armed forces' actual characteristics and conditions, as well as to the wars they are likely to fight. For instance, the attack on the Saudi oil processing facility in September 2019 called attention to the dearth of properly placed and operated medium-range air defense systems designed to intercept cruise missiles and unmanned aerial vehicles (i.e., drones; Helou 2019b). Building up air power at the expense of navies and other security needs is something that will have to be rectified in the Gulf in the coming years. The GCC countries' collective capacity to operate and maintain their armaments must correspond to the technological sophistication of those weapons. The near-total reliance of most Gulf states on international allies for even basic requirements of national defense, like weapons maintenance, ought to be reduced by prioritizing the training of local personnel.

In the economic sphere, the Gulf states must restructure and diversify their economies and reduce waste. Areas in the Gulf countries' defense establishments where serious money could be saved are legion. The biggest potential savings are connected to armament acquisition. Actual need and pragmatic consideration ought to drive decisions to purchase this or that weapon system, practices that encourage corruption must be weeded out, and the entire concept behind the development of indigenous defense industries needs to be reassessed. A significant proportion of the Gulf militaries' arsenal is in poor condition simply because weapons and equipment are inappropriately or insufficiently maintained and serviced. Implementing and adhering to maintenance protocols required by manufacturers would extend the life of armaments and make their frequent replacement unnecessary. Fast-depreciating surplus gear and supplies should be sold off. The stovepipe-like rank structure of Gulf armies is also financially wasteful, as a large number of redundant senior officers continue to draw generous salaries and benefits. Rationalizing the rank structure by transforming it to resemble a pyramid would be rewarded by significant savings.

The social contract between the rulers and the ruled in the Gulf monarchies has long been based on the monarchies' generous subsidies on everything from housing and education to utilities and water in exchange for no political rights. With the expected long-term decline in the world market price of hydrocarbons – a recent study by British Petroleum argues that the relentless growth of oil demand is over (British Petroleum 2020) – GCC states will have to drastically revise the terms of this contract. In order to forestall social upheaval and maintain their rule, the absolute monarchies will likely need to consider a gradual shift toward constitutional monarchies – a difficult process seldom accomplished peacefully (Huntington 1966: 783) – extending civil rights to their citizens to compensate for the economic benefits they will no longer be able to provide.

References

Abdulaal, Abdulla. 2015. "Bahrain's Opportunity for Economic Reform," *Sada – Carnegie Endowment for International Peace*, April 10.

Abul-Magd, Zeinab. 2017. *Militarizing the Nation: The Army, Business, and Revolution in Egypt* (New York: Columbia University Press).

AFP. 2019. "Qatar Opens Its Largest Coast Guard Base," July 14.

Alajmi, Zafer Muhammad. 2015. "Gulf Military Cooperation: Tangible Gains or Limited Results?," in Jamal Abdullah, ed., *Gulf Cooperation Council's Challenges and Prospects* (Doha: Al Jazeera Center for Studies), 47–58.

Al Defaiya. 2017a. "Egypt Takes Part in Joint Military Drills with Bahrain, UAE," March 13.

Al Defaiya. 2017b. "Saudi Arabia to Acquire Australian Military Equipment," March 30.

Al Defaiya. 2017c. "Saudi Arabia to Build Major Aerospace Facility," June 6.

Al Defaiya. 2017d. "Royal Air Force of Oman Receives 1st Hawk Jet Trainers," August 2.

Al Defaiya. 2017e. "Qatar, France Ink $14 Billion Military, Aviation Deals," December 11.

Al Defaiya. 2018a. "Saudi Arabia to Host Armed Forces Exhibition – AFED 2018," February 20.

Al Defaiya. 2018b. "Germany Approves Arms Sales to Gulf, Mideast Countries," September 26.

Al Defaiya. 2019. "Qatar Orders Two Large Aircraft Infrared Countermeasure Systems," September 26.

Amlôt, Matthew. 2020. "Russian State Nuclear Firm Advances in Bid Process for Saudi Project," *Al-Arabiya*, February 10.

Andolu. 2019. "Qatar First to Buy US-Made AMRAAM-ER Missiles," July 11.

Anthony, John Duke. 2016. "GCC Arms Imports: Strategic Assessment and Economic Benefits to the United States," in David B. Des Roches and Dania Thafer, eds., *The Arms Trade, Military Services, and the Security Market in the Gulf States: Trends and Implications* (Berlin: Gerlach, 2016), 23–43.

Asharq Al-Awsat. 2019. "Kuwait Emir: No One Can Evade Punishment for Corruption," November 18.

Ashri, Osama. 2019. "On the Fast Track: Saudi Arabia's Entrepreneurship Ecosystem," *Entrepreneur Middle East*, July 17.

Askari, Hossein, Amin Mohseni, and Shahrzad Daneshvar. 2009. *The Militarization of the Persian Gulf: An Economic Analysis* (Northampton: Edward Elgar).

Assl, Nima Khorrami. 2018. "Oman's Economic Ambitions," Sada, *Carnegie Endowment for International Peace (CEIP)*, December 14.

Ayubi, Nazih N. 1995. *Over-Stating the Arab State: Politics and Society in the Middle East* (London: I. B. Tauris).

Bahgat, Gawdat. 1995. "Military Security and Political Stability in the Gulf," *Arab Studies Quarterly*, 17:4 (Fall): 55–70.

Bahgat, Gawdat. 2008. *Proliferation of Nuclear Weapons in the Middle East* (Gainesville: University Press of Florida).

Bahgat, Gawdat. 2016. "Lower for Longer: Saudi Arabia Adjusts to the New Oil Era," *Middle East Policy*, 23:3 (Fall): 39–48.

Bahgat, Gawdat. 2017. "The Emerging Energy Landscape: Economic and Strategic Implications," in Kristian Coates Ulrichsen, ed., *The Changing Security Dynamics of the Persian Gulf* (New York: Oxford University Press), 61–76.

Barany, Zoltan. 2012. *The Soldier and the Changing State: Building Democratic Armies in Africa, Asia, Europe, and the Americas* (Princeton, NJ: Princeton University Press).

Barany, Zoltan. 2013. "Unrest and State Response in the Arab Monarchies," *Mediterranean Quarterly*, 24:2 (Spring): 5–38.

Barany, Zoltan. 2018. "Why Have Three Gulf States Introduced the Draft? Bucking the Trend on Conscription in Arabia," *RUSI Journal* (Royal United Services Institute), 162:6 (January): 16–27.

Barany, Zoltan. 2019. "Military Politics and Foreign Policy-Making: Changing Dynamics in North African Regimes," *Journal of North African Studies*, 24:4 (July): 592–598.

Barany, Zoltan. 2020a. "Foreign Contract Soldiers in the Gulf," *Carnegie Middle East Center*, February 5.

Barany, Zoltan. 2020b. "Arms Procurement and Corruption in the Gulf Monarchies," Burke Chair Report, *Center for Strategic and International Studies*, May 11.

Barany, Zoltan. forthcoming. "The Gulf Monarchies and Israel: From Aversion to Pragmatism," *Middle East Journal*.

Barr, Abigail, and Danila Serra. 2010. "Corruption and Culture: An Experimental Analysis," *Journal of Public Economics*, 94:11–12 (December 2010): 862–869.

Batrawy, Aya. 2020. "New Oman Ruler Vows to Uphold Late Sultan's Peaceful Policy," *AP* (Dubai), January 11.

Bendix, Reinhard. 1980. *Kings or People: Power and the Mandate to Rule* (Berkeley: University of California Press).

Bianco, Cinzia, and Giorgio Cafiero. 2016. "The Price Bahrain Pays for Saudi Assistance," *Lobe Log*, May 4.

Bianco, Cinzia, and Gareth Stansfield. 2018. "The Intra-GCC Crises: Mapping GCC Fragmentation after 2011," *International Affairs*, 94:3: 613–635.

Binnie, Jeremy. 2019. "Saudi Air Defences Are Ill-Prepared for Low-Level Attacks," *HIS Markit*, September 28.

Blanchard, Christopher M. 2016. *Saudi Arabia: Background and U.S. Relations* (Washington, DC: Congressional Research Service, April 22).

Borchert, Heiko. "The Arab Gulf Defense Pivot: Defense Industrial Policy in a Changing Geostrategic Context," *Comparative Strategy*, 37:4 (2018): 299–315.

Boughanmi, Houcine, and Muhammad Aamir Khan. 2019. "Welfare and Distributional Effects of the Energy Subsidy Reform in the Gulf Cooperation Council Countries," *International Journal of Energy Economics and Policy*, 9:1: 228–236.

Bove, Vincenzo, and Jennifer Brauner. 2016. "The Demand for Military Expenditure in Authoritarian Regimes," *Defense and Peace Economics*, 27:5: 609–625.

British Petroleum. 2020. "Energy Outlook," September 14, available at www .bp.com/en/global/corporate/energy-economics/energy-outlook.html.

Brooks, Risa A. 2003. "Making Military Might: Why Do States Fail or Succeed: A Review Essay," *International Security*, 28:2 (Fall): 149–191.

Brown, Gordon S., and Kenneth Katzman. 2001. "Gulf Cooperation Council Defense Agreement," *CRS Report for Congress* (Washington, DC: Congressional Research Service), February 28.

Cahill, Ben. 2020. "Gulf States: Managing the Oil Crash," *Center for Strategic and International Studies Commentary*, May 7.

Cannon, Brendon J., and Ash Rossiter. 2017. "Ethiopia, Berbera Port, and the Shifting Balance of Power in the Horn of Africa," *Rising Powers Quarterly*, 2:4 (December): 7–29.

Carey, Glen. 2018. "Saudis Want to Make Their Own Weapons. Russia Is Eager to Help," *Bloomberg*, March 2.

Castelier, Sebastian, and Quentin Müller. 2019. "Oman's Duqm, a New Port City for the Middle East?" *Middle East Eye*, February 10.

CB Insights. 2017. "The Kingdom of Tech: Mapping Saudi Arabia's Investors and Their Startup Bets," March 9.

Chehabi, H. E., and Juan J. Linz. 1998. "A Theory of Sultanism 1: A Type of Nondemocratic Rule," in Chehabi and Linz, eds., *Sultanistic Regimes* (Baltimore: Johns Hopkins University Press), 3–25.

Coates Ulrichsen, Kristian. 2020. *Qatar and the Gulf Crisis* (New York: Oxford University Press).

Congressional Research Service. 2020. "Congress and the War in Yemen: Oversight and Legislation 2015–2020," *Congressional Research Service*, R45046, June 19.

Cordesman, Anthony H. 2010. *Gulf Military Balance* (Washington, DC: CSIS).

Cordesman, Anthony H. (with the assistance of Bryan Gold and Garrett Berntsen). 2014. *The Gulf Military Balance: Vol. 1: The Conventional and Assymmetric Dimensions* (Boulder: Rowman & Littlefield/CSIS).

Cordesman, Anthony H. 2018. "Military Spending: The Other Side of Saudi Security," Burke Chair Report, *Center for Strategic and International Studies* (henceforth, *CSIS*), March 11.

Cordesman, Anthony H., Robert M. Shelala, and Omar Mohamed. 2014. *The Gulf Military Balance: Vol. 3: The Gulf and the Arabian Peninsula* (Boulder: Rowman & Littlefield/CSIS).

Cronin, Stephanie. 2014. *Armies and State-Building in the Modern Middle East* (London: I. B. Tauris).

Davids, Gavin. 2013. "Construction the Most Corrupt Industry in Arab Countries," *ME Construction News*, September 9.

Davidson, Christopher M. 2008. *Dubai: The Vulnerability of Success* (New York: Columbia University Press).

De Atkine, Norvell B. 2000. "Why Arabs Lose Wars," *Middle East Review of International Affairs*, 4:1 (March): 16–27.

De Atkine, Norvell B. 2013. "Western Influence on Arab Militaries: Pounding Square Pegs into Round Holes," *Middle East Review of International Affairs*, 17:1 (Spring): 18–31.

Defense News. 2019. "Will the UAE Buy Russia Su-57, Su 35 Jets?" November 18, the video report is available at www.defensenews.com/video/2019/11/18/will-the-uae-buy-russian-su-57-su-35-jets-dubai-air show–2019/.

Defense Security Cooperation Agency. 2019. "UAE to Receive 10 CH-47F Chinook Cargo Helicopters," November 11.

Des Roches, David B. 2017. "US Military Interests in the Arab Region: Sales, Stability, and Security," in Zeina Azzam and Imad K. Harb, eds., *Trump and the Arab World: A First Year Assessment* (Washington, DC: Arab Center), 19–28.

Dourian, Kate. 2019. "Oman: A Small Oil Player with Big Ambitions," *Arabian Gulf Studies Institute Washington* (henceforth *AGSIW*), November 7.

Doward, Jamie. 2020. "UK Accused of Selling Arms to Saudi Arabia a Year after Court Ban," *Guardian*, June 21.

Economist. 2015. "Full of Sound and Fury," *Economist*, August 22, 39.

Economist. 2017. "Qatar and Its Neighbours: Economic Gulf," October 21, 49.

Economist. 2018a. "A Wild Ride," *Special Report on the Gulf*, June 23, 4.

Economist. 2018b. "Where Are the Jobs for the Boys?," November 24.

Economist. 2018c. "A Prince Fails to Charm," December 22, 74.

Economist. 2019a. "Weapon Sales: Predator Pricing," March 9, 43–44.

Economist. 2019b. "Bahrain: A Gulf Case Study," May 25, 45.

Economist. 2019c. "Sovereign Wealth, Sovereign Whims," June 15, 40.

Economist. 2020. "Twilight of an Era: The End of the Arab World's Oil-Age Is Night," July 18, 37.

Edmondson, Catie. 2020. "House Votes to Block Arms Sales to Gulf Nations, Setting Up Trump's Third Veto," *New York Times*, July 17.

Ellyatt, Holly. 2019. "Saudi Arabia Is 'Gradually Running Out of Money' and Needs IPO to Fund Reforms, Ex-CIA Chief Says," *CNBC.com*, November 14.

Ennis, Crystal A., and Ra'id Z. al-Jamali. 2014. "Elusive Employment Development Planning and Labour Market Trends in Oman," *Middle East and North Africa Research Paper* (Chatham House), September.

Entous, Adam. 2018. "The Enemy of My Enemy," *New Yorker*, June 18, 30–45.

Exum, Andrew. 2019. "U.S. Arms Sales to the Gulf Have Failed," *Atlantic*, June 21.

Farooq, Khalid, and Graham Brooks. 2013. "Arab Fraud and Corruption Professionals' Views in the Arabian Gulf," *Journal of Financial Crime*, 20:3: 338–347.

Farzegan, Mohammad Reza. 2018. "The Impact of Oil Rents on Military Spending in the GCC Region: Does Corruption Matter?" *Journal of Arabian Studies*, 8: CIRS Special Issue: 87–109.

Fathallah, Hadi. 2019. "The Economic Consequences of Gulf Insecurity," Sada, *CEIP*, September 11.

Fingar, Courtney. 2018. "Kuwaiti Economy Needs Foreign Investment to Diversify," *Financial Times*, September 10.

Fishman, Brian. 2016. *The Master Plan: ISIS, Al Qaeda, and the Jihadi Strategy for Final Victory* (New Haven, CT: Yale University Press).

Gaub, Florence. 2017. *Guardians of the Arab State* (London: C. Hurst & Co.).

Gaub, Florence, and Zoe Stanley-Lockman. 2017. "Defence Industries in Arab States: Player and Strategies," *Chaillot Paper* No. 141 (European Union Institute for Security Studies, March).

Gengler, Justin. 2020. "Will Saudi Arabia Cut Funding to MbS's Costly Misadventures?" *Responsible Statecraft*, May 15.

Al-Ghanim, Mohammed. 2010. "Do Elections Lead to Reform? Assessing the Institutional Limits of Representative Bodies in Bahrain, Kuwait, and Saudi Arabia," *Contemporary Arab Affairs*, 3:2: 138–147.

Giunchi, Elisa Ada. 2014. "The Political and Economic Role of the Pakistani Military," *ISPI* (Italian Institute for International Political Studies) *Analysis*, no. 269, July.

Gordon, Philip H., Michael Doran, and Jon B. Alterman. 2019. "The Trump Administration's Middle East Policies: A Mid-term Assessment," *Middle East Policy*, 26:1 (Spring): 5–30.

Gray, Matthew. 2019. *The Economy of the Gulf States*. (Newcastle: Agenda).

Grimm, Jannis Julien. 2019. "Egypt Is Not for Sale! Harnessing Nationalism for Alliance Building in Egypt's Tiran and Sanafir Island Protests," *Mediterranean Politics*, 24:4: 443–466.

Guardian. 2017. "Saudi Prince Miteb bin Abdullah Pays $1bn in Corruption Settlement," November 29.

Gulf News. 2015. "BDF Signs $56 Million Healthcare Project Agreement with KMC," September 20.

Guzansky, Yoel. 2016. "Lines Drawn in the Sand: Territorial Disputes and GCC Unity," *Middle East Journal*, 70:4 (Autumn): 543–559.

Hanieh, Adam. 2018. *Money, Markets, and Monarchies: The Gulf Cooperation Council and the Political Economy of the Contemporary Middle East* (Cambridge: Cambridge University Press).

Harb, Imad K. 2017. "The United States and the GCC: A Steep Learning Curve for President Trump," in Zeina Azzam and Imad K. Harb, eds. *Trump and the Arab World: A First Year Assessment* (Washington, DC: Arab Center, 2017), 49–56.

Hasbani, Nadim. 2006. "The Geopolitics of Weapons Procurement in the Gulf States," *Defense & Security Analysis*, 22:1 (March): 73–88.

Al-Hashemi, Mohammed Hashem. 2019. "Bitter Brethren: Freud's Narcissism of Minor Differences and the Gulf Divide," in Andreas Krieg, ed., *Divided Gulf: The Anatomy of a Crisis* (Singapore: Palgrave Macmillan 2019), 53–70.

El-Hassen, Tarek, and Hamid Al Bilali. 2019. "Food Security in the Gulf Cooperation Council Countries: Challenges and Prospects," *Journal of Food Security*, 7:5: 159–169.

Haykel, Bernard. 2016. "ISIS and al-Qaeda – What Are They Thinking? Understanding the Adversary," *The ANNALS of the American Academy of Political and Social Science*, 668:1 (November): 71–81.

Hearst, David. 2018. "With Matthew Hedges, the UAE Is Up to Its Old Bullying Games," *Middle East Eye*, December 2.

Heath, Victoria. 2016. "Defense Gaps in the GCC: A Case Study of Saudi Arabia and the Royal Saudi Air Force," in David B. Des Roches and Dania Thafer, eds., *The Arms Trade, Military Services and the Security Market in the Gulf States: Trends and Implications* (Berlin: Gerlach Press), 80–98.

Helou, Agnes. 2019a. "UAE Launches 'Edge' Conglomerate to Address Its 'Antiquated Military Industry,'" *Defense News*, November 6.

Helou, Agnes. 2019b. "How Can Saudi Arabia Secure Its Airspace?," *Defense News*, November 15.

Helou, Agnes 2020. "Amid Western Arms Embargoes on Saudi Arabia, SAMI Has a Backup Plan," *Defense News*, January 14.

Herb, Michael. 1999. *All in the Family: Absolutism, Revolution, and Democracy in Middle Eastern Monarchies* (Albany: SUNY Press).

Herb, Michael. 2004. "Princes and Parliaments of the Arab World," *Middle East Journal*, 58:3 (July): 367–384.

Hirst, David. 2017. "Senior Saudi Figures Tortured and Beaten in Purge," *Middle East Eye*, November 10.

Hubbard, Ben. 2016. "Saudis Cut off Funding for Military Aid to Lebanon," *New York Times*, February 20.

Hungtington, Samuel P. 1966. "The Political Modernization of Traditional Monarchies," *Daedalus*, 95:3 (Summer): 763–788.

Ibish, Hussein. 2017. "The UAE's Evolving National Security Strategy," Issue Paper No. 4, *Arab Gulf States Institute in Washington*, April 6.

IISS (International Institute for Strategic Studies). 2019. *The Military Balance 2019* (London: IISS).

IISS Strategic Comments. 2013. "Equipment Purchases Boost Gulf Defences," 19:34 (November).

Insinna, Valerie. 2019a. "US Puts F-35 Talks with the UAE on the Backburner to Focus on F-16 Upgrades," *Defense News*, November 17.

Insinna, Valerie. 2019b. "Calidus Inks Its First B-250 Light Attack Plane Order," *Defense News*, November 20.

Jarzabek, Jarosław. 2016. "GCC Military Spending in Era of Low Oil Prices," *Middle East Institute*, Policy Focus Series, August.

Al Jazeera. 2019. "Kuwait's Emir: Gulf Dispute 'No Longer Acceptable or Tolerable,'" October 29.

Juneau, Thomas. 2016. "Iran's Policy Towards the Houthis in Yemen: A Limited Return on a Modest Investment," *International Affairs*, 92:3 (May): 647–663.

Kalin, Stephen. 2020. "Saudi Crown Prince Barrels Ahead with Big Projects to Boost Economy," *Wall Street Journal*, August 26.

Kamrava, Mehran. 2018. *Troubled Waters: Insecurity in the Persian Gulf* (Ithaca, NY: Cornell University Press).

Kassan, Ashifa. 2018. "Justin Trudeau Defends Canada's Arms Sales to Saudi Arabia," *Guardian*, March 21.

Kéchichian, Joseph. 2001. *Succession in Saudi Arabia* (New York: Palgrave-Macmillan).

Khaleej Times. 2012. "Tawazun Inks JV for Nimr Manufacturing in Algeria," July 29.

Al-Khamri, Hana. 2019. "Vision 2030 and Poverty in Saudi Arabia," *Al Jazeera*, December 23.

Khan, Ghazanfar Ali. 2017. "Saudi Arabia Seeks to Build Robust Defense Industry," *Arab News*, February 26.

Kirkpatrick, David D., and Ben Hubbard. 2020. "Saudi Prince Detains Senior Members of Royal Family," *New York Times*, March 6.

Krane, Jim. 2019a. "Subsidy Reform and Tax Increases in the Rentier Middle East," in *The Politics of the Rentier States in the Gulf* (Washington, DC: Project on Middle East Political Science (www.pomeps.org), January 18–24.

Krane, Jim. 2019b. *Energy Kingdoms: Oil and Political Survival in the Persian Gulf* (New York: Columbia University Press).

Kuimova, Alexandra. 2020. "Understanding Egyptian Military Expenditure," *SIPRI Background Paper*, October.

Kulish, Nicholas, and David D. Kirkpatrick. 2017. "In Saudi Arabia, Where Family and State Are One, Arrests May Be Selective," *New York Times*, November 7.

Kulish, Nicholas, and Mark Mazzetti. 2016. "Saudi Royal Family Is Still Spending in an Age of Austerity," *New York Times*, December 27.

Legrenzi, Matteo. 2011. *The GCC and the International Relations of the Gulf* (London: I. B. Tauris).

Lucas, Russell. 2004. "Monarchical Authoritarianism: Survival and Political Liberalization in a Middle Eastern Regime Type," *International Journal of Middle East Studies*, 36:1 (February): 103–119.

Mandour, Maged. 2016. "Egypt's Shift from Saudi Arabia to Russia," Sada, *CEIP*, November 3.

Marchi, Vivienne. 2018. "Qatar Navy Expansion Continues with New Ships and Bases by 2022," *Defense Daily*, November 28.

Marshall, Shana. 2010. "The Modernization of Bribery: The Arms Trade in the Arab Gulf," *Jadaliyya*, December 22.

Marshall, Shana. 2016. "Military Prestige, Defense-Industrial Production, and the Rise of Gulf Military Activism," in Holger Albrecht, Aurel Croissant, and Fred H. Lawson, eds., *Armies and Insurgencies in the Arab Spring* (Philadelphia: University of Pennsylvania Press, 2016), 241–263.

Matthiesen, Toby. 2013. *Sectarian Gulf: Bahrain, Saudi Arabia, and the Arab Spring That Wasn't* (Stanford, CA: Stanford University Press).

Mazzetti, Mark, and Emily B. Hager. 2011. "Secret Desert Force Set Up by Blackwater's Founder," *New York Times*, May 14.

McDowall, Angus, Phil Stewart, and David Rohde. 2016. "Yemen's Guerrilla War Tests Military Ambitions of Big-Spending Saudis," *Reuters*, April 19.

Merat, Arron. 2019. "'The Saudis Couldn't Do It without Us': The UK's True Role in Yemen's Deadly War," *Guardian*, June 18.

Merrill, Jamie. 2016. "Major British Defense Deal with Oman Comes Under Fire," *Middle East Eye*, May 20.

Middle East Eye. 2020. "Saudi King Removes Commander of Yemen Force over Corruption Claims," *Middle East Eye*, August 31.

Naar, Ismaeel. 2020. "Saudi Arabia's Anti-Corruption Authority Opens 218 Criminal Cases," *Al Arabiya*, August 11.

Naidu, Suresh, Yaw Nyarko, and Shing-Yi Wang. 2016 "Monopsony Power in Migrant Labor Markets: Evidence from the United Arab Emirates," *Journal of Political Economy*, 124:6 (December): 1735–1792.

National (UAE). 2017. "Saudi Arabia, UAE Form Military Alliance," December 7.

Niarchos, Nicholas. 2018. "Making War: How U.S. Support Inflames the Conflict in Yemen," *New Yorker*, January 22, 30–35.

Obouzzohour, Yasmina. "As Oman Enters a New Era, Economic and Political Challenges Persist," Order from Chaos, *Brookings*, January 15.

Al Omran, Ahmed, and Peggy Hollinger. 2018. "Saudi Arabia Beefs Up Plans for Domestic Defence Industry," *Financial Times*, March 15.

Page, Matthew T., and Jodi Vittori, eds. 2020. *Dubai's Role in Facilitating Corruption and Global Illicit Financial Flows* (Washington, DC: Carnegie Endowment for International Peace, 2020).

Partrick, Neil. 2018. "Saudi Arabia's Elusive Defense Reform," Sada, *CEIP*, May 31.

Partrick, Neil. 2019. "Saudi Economic Reforms: Shadows and Light," *neilpartrick.com*, November 18.

Pérez-Peña, Richard. 2018. "Britain to Sell Jets to Saudis Despite Conduct of Yemen War," *New York Times*, March 9.

Peterson, J. E. 2018. "Prospects for Proliferation in Saudi Arabia," in Jeannie L. Johnson, Kerry M. Kartchner, and Marilyn J. Maines, eds., *Crossing Nuclear Thresholds: Leveraging Sociocultural Insights into Nuclear Decisionmaking* (New York: Palgrave Macmillan), 109–139.

Pollack, Kenneth M. 2019. *Armies of Sand: The Past, Present, and Future of Arab Military Effectiveness* (New York: Oxford University Press).

Porter, Geoff D. 2019. "Political Instability in Algeria," Center for Preventive Action, Contingency Planning Memorandum No. 35.

Qatar News Agency. "Qatar to Build New Air Base," August 30, 2018.

Quinlivan, James T. 1999. "Coup-Proofing: Its Practice and Consequences in the Middle East," *International Security*, 24:2 (Fall): 131–165.

Reporters without Borders. 2019. *2019 World Press Freedom Index*, https://rsf.org/en/ranking.

Reuters. 2015."Saudi Security Spending Rises $5.3 Bln in 2015: Minister," December 28.

Reuters. 2016. "Dutch Parliament Votes to Ban Weapons Exports to Saudi Arabia," March 15.

Reuters. 2018a. "Saudi Economist Who Criticized Aramco IPO Charged with Terrorism," October 1.

Reuters. 2018b. "Under Saudi Threat, Qatar Ramps Up Major Air and Sea Power Buildup," November 29.

Reuters. 2019. "Bahrain's Crown Prince Signs Deal to Buy Patriot Missiles," September 16.

Reuters. 2020a. "Saudi-Qatar Talks to End Lengthy Gulf Dispute Falter" (Dubai), February 11.

Reuters. 2020b. "Bailed-Out Bahrain May Need More Gulf Support as Soon as This Year" (Dubai), May 4.

Riedel, Bruce. 2017a. "The $110 Billion Arms Deal to Saudi Arabia Is Fake News," Markaz, *Brookings*, June 5.

Riedel, Bruce. 2017b. "In Yemen Iran Outsmarts Saudi Arabia, Again," Markaz, *Brookings Institution*, December 6.

Riedel, Bruce. 2018. *Kings and Presidents: Saudi Arabia and the United States since FDR* (Washington, DC: Brookings).

Roberts, David B. 2019. "Reflecting on Qatar's 'Islamist' Soft Power," Policy Brief, *Brookings Foreign Policy Program*, April.

Roeber, Joe. 2005. "Parallel Markets: Corruption in the International Arms Trade," Goodwin Paper No. 3 (London: Campaign Against Arms Trade, June 2005).

Roll, Stephan. 2019. "A Sovereign Wealth Fund for the Prince," *SWP Research Paper* No. 8 (Berlin: Stiftung Wissenschaft und Politik, July).

Russell, Richard L. 2009. "Future Gulf War: Arab and American Forces against Iranian Capabilities," *Joint Force Quarterly*, 55:4: 35–40.

Sabbagh, Dan. 2020. "Britain to Resume Sale of Arms to Saudi Arabia Despite Yemen Fears," *Guardian*, July 7.

Sailer, Matthias. 2016. "Changed Priorities in the Gulf," *SWP Comments* No. 8, January.

Salama, Samir. 2020. "Saudi Arabia Set to Manufacture New Armoured Military Vehicle," *Gulf News*, July 2.

Samaan, Jean-Loup Samaan. 2019. "The Rise of the Emirate Defense Industry," Sada, *CEIP*, May 14.

Sanger, David E., and William J. Broad. 2018. "Saudis Want a U.S. Nuclear Deal," *New York Times*, November 22.

Saudi-US Trade Group.com. 2020. "Coming Soon to Saudi Arabia: A 'World Defense Show' to Rival Abu Dhabi's IDEX," July 17.

Schwartz, Felicia. 2020. "Possible F-35 Jet Sale to U.A.E. Puts Israel in Bind," *Wall Street Journal*, August 20.

Serra, Danila. 2006. "Empirical Determinants of Corruption: A Sensitivity Analysis," *Public Choice*, 126 (January): 225–256.

Al Sherbini, Ramadan. 2020. "In First, Kuwait Ex-Minister Gets Jail Sentence," *Gulf News*, January 29.

SIPRI (Stockholm International for Peace Research Institute). 2017. "Trends in World Military Expenditure, 2017," SIPRI Fact Sheet (Stockholm, May).

SIPRI. 2019a. *SIPRI Yearbook 2019: Armaments, Disarmament and International Security* (Oxford: Oxford University Press).

SIPRI. 2019b. "World's 10 Largest Defense Companies," December 31.

Soubrier, Emma. 2016. "Mirages of Power? From Sparkly Appearances to Empowered Apparatus, Evolving Trends and Implications of Arms Trade in Qatar and the UAE," David B. Des Roches and Dania Thafer, eds., *The Arms Trade, Military Services and the Security Market in the Gulf States: Trends and Implications* (Berlin: Gerlach Press), 135–151.

Soubrier, Emma. 2019. "Air Power Procurement in the Gulf: From Sparkling Mirages to Strategic Ambitions," *Arabian Gulf Studies Institute Washington*, December 6.

Sprenger, Sebastian. 2020. "Saab Delivers First Global Eye Early-Warning Plane to UAE," *Defense News*, April 29.

Stanley, Bruce, and Heesu Lee. 2018. "UAE Completes First of Four Korean-Built Nuclear Reactors," *Bloomberg*, March 26.

Stanley-Lockman, Zoe. 2017. "The UAE's Defense Horizons," Sada, *CEIP*, May 2.

Stone, Jon. 2018. "Germany, Denmark, Netherlands, and Finland Stop Weapons Sales to Saudi Arabia in Response to Yemen Famine," *Independent*, November 23.

Al-Sulami, Mohammed. 2019. "Localization of Saudi Military Industry to Support Economic Diversification," *Arab News*, November 11.

Sutton, H. I. 2020. "Qatar to Acquire Submarines in New Twist in Gulf States' Big Naval Expansion," *Forbes*, February 4.

Tabrizi, Aniseh Bassiri, and Justin Bronk. 2018. *Armed Drones in the Middle East: Proliferation and Norms in the Region, RUSI Occasional Paper* (London: Royal United Services Institute, December).

TASS. 2017. "UAE Wants to Buy Over a Squadron of Su-35 Advanced Fighter Jets from Russia" (Moscow), October 3.

Van Brunnersum, Melissa Sou-Jie. 2020. "Germany Violated Arms Export Regulations for Decades, Study Says," *Deutsche Welle*, July 19.

Wahid, Latif. 2009. *Military Expenditure and Economic Grown in the Middle East* (New York: Palgrave Macmillan).

Walsh, Declan. 2017. "Qatar Buys Italian Warships as Persian Gulf Crisis Deepens," *New York Times*, August 2.

Walsh, Declan, and Eric Schmitt. 2018. "Arms Sales to Saudis Leave American Fingerprints on Yemen's Carnage," *New York Times*, December 25.

Wearing, David. 2018. *AngloArabia: Why Gulf Wealth Matters to Britain* (Cambridge: Polity, 2018).

Wehrey, Frederic M. 2014. *Sectarian Politics in the Gulf: From the Iraq War to the Arab Uprisings* (New York: Columbia University Press).

Weisgerber, Marcus. 2019. "Saudi Losses in Yemen War Exposed by US Tank Deal," *Defense One*, August 9.

Wheatcroft, Andrew. 1995. *The Life and Times of Shaikh Salman bin Hamad Al-Khalifa, Ruler of Bahrain 1942–1961* (London: Kegan Paul International).

Whynes, David. 1979. *The Economics of Third World Military Expenditure* (London: Macmillan).

Wiegand, Krista E. 2012. "Bahrain, Qatar, and the Hawar Islands: Resolution of a Gulf Territorial Dispute," *Middle East Journal*, 66:1 (Winter): 79–96.

Winder, Bayly. 2020. "Next in Line: Succession and the Kuwaiti Monarchy," *Carnegie Endowment for International Peace*, August 13.

Wolf, Albert. 2020. "The UAE-Israel Agreement Isn't All It's Cracked Up to Be," *Foreign Policy*, August 15.

Wolf, Anne. 2019. "Saudi Arabia Reasserts Itself in the Maghrib," *Journal of North African Studies*, 24:4: 533–539.

Wolverton, Joe. 2019. "China Set to Sell Weaponized Drones to Saudi Arabia," *New American*, November 21.

Wright, Robin. 2018. "Can Saudi Arabia's Crown Prince, Mohammed bin Salman, Survive the Jamal Khashoggi Murder?" *New Yorker*, October 25.

Younes, Ali. 2019. "Qatar's New Naval Base to 'Address Security, Protect Assets,'" *Al Jazeera*, July 14.

Young, Karen. 2019a. "UAE Diversification Strategy Lags Despite Growth in Oil Sector," *Al-Monitor*, August 6.

Young, Karen. 2019b. "Sell-off in Oman Reveals Privatization with Regional Characteristics," *Al-Monitor*, December 27.

Acknowledgments

I am grateful to Omar Al-Ubaydli and the anonymous reviewers for their insightful comments and to Keith Hartley for his valuable suggestions and for shepherding the manuscript through the publication process.

About the Author

Zoltan Barany is the Frank C. Erwin, Jr. Centennial Professor of Government at the University of Texas. His books include *How Armies Respond to Revolutions and Why* (Princeton University Press, 2016), *The Soldier and the Changing State: Building Democratic Armies in Africa, Asia, Europe, and the Americas* (Princeton University Press, 2012), and, as co-editor, *Is Democracy Exportable?* (Cambridge University Press, 2009), all of which have been translated in to Arabic. His next book, *Armies of Arabia: Military Politics and Effectiveness in the Gulf* is forthcoming from Oxford University Press.

Cambridge Elements ⹀

Defence Economics

Keith Hartley
University of York

Keith Hartley was Professor of Economics and Director of the Centre for Defence Economics at the University of York, where he is now Emeritus Professor of Economics. He is the author of over 500 publications comprising journal articles, books and reports. His most recent books include *The Economics of Arms* (Agenda Publishing, 2017) and with Jean Belin (Eds) *The Economics of the Global Defence Industry* (Taylor and Francis, 2020). Hartley was founding Editor of the journal *Defence and Peace Economics*; a NATO Research Fellow; a QinetiQ Visiting Fellow; consultant to the UN, EC, EDA, UK MoD, HM Treasury, Trade and Industry, Business, Innovation and Skills and International Development and previously Special Adviser to the House of Commons Defence Committee.

About the Series

Defence Economics is a relatively new field within the discipline of economics. It studies all aspects of the economics of war and peace. It embraces a wide range of topics in both macroeconomics and microeconomics. Cambridge Elements in Defence Economics aims to publish original and authoritative papers in the field. These will include expert surveys of the foundations of the discipline, its historical development and contributions developing new and novel topics. They will be valuable contributions to both research and teaching in universities and colleges, and will also appeal to other specialist groups comprising politicians, military and industrial personnel as well as informed general readers.

Cambridge Elements ≡

Defence Economics

Elements in the Series

Defence Economics: Achievements and Challenges
Keith Hartley

The Political Economy of Gulf Defense Establishments
Zoltan Barany

A full series listing is available at: www.cambridge.org/EDEC